COMMON SENSE SUCCESS

COMMON SENSE SUCCESS

A Refresher Course on the Fundamentals of Business and Life

BILL ARNOLD

Inukshuk Success Press
DALLAS, TEXAS

Read the common sense success blog at
www.commonsensesuccess.net

Common Sense Success: A refresher course on the fundamentals of business and life
Bill Arnold

ISBN 978-0-615-23205-8

Published by Inukshuk Success Press, in association with Bill Arnold

For book ordering information or to book an engagment with Bill Arnold:
Inukshuk Success Press:
1586 Main Street, Southlake, TX 76092
Email: *info@commonsensesuccess.net*
817.366.9671

For more information on *Common Sense Success,* go to *www.commonsensesuccess.net.*

Edited by Philip Holsinger. Book design by Brandon Tittle and Philip Holsinger.
On the cover: In ancient times Innuit Indians erected rock cairns for use as navigation devices in the formless arctic landscape. The markers resembled a person and would, with one "arm" extended longer, point the way to home, to a cache of food, or to the nourishment of the hunting ground. Commonly called inukshuks, they came to symbolize the hope of direction in life. Modern rock cairn and photo by Philip Holsinger.

For Those Who Seek

CONTENTS

FIRST WORDS

Finding Your Way

In ancient times Inuit Indians stacked rocks in the formless arctic landscape for use as navigation markers. Over time the markers came to resemble a person and would, with one "arm" extended longer on one side, point the way home, to a cache of food, or to the nourishment of the hunting ground. Commonly called inukshuk, the markers came to symbolize direction in life.

That is what this book is about: direction. We may not be traveling across a barren arctic landscape today, but with all the noise and clutter of this present age it is just as easy to lose our way. Think of this book as an inukshuk pointing the way toward the things in life you may have strayed from, a little stack of rocks marking a path among the noise and clutter, helping to guide your way.

I have been both the employee in search of success and the employer in search of employees hungering for success. In more than forty years in the workplace I have seen a lot of different kinds of people and seen people of all types succeed and fail. There is one basic difference between those who succeed and those who fail: those who succeed simply determine not to quit.

There, I've told you what I know. Now you may not want to read this book. Success in my book is as common sense as this: don't quit.

But it is more than not quitting. It is maintaining dignity and self-respect while you determine to keep going. It is getting back up after a failure and trying again. It is developing character and developing skills for understanding and getting along with others. It is learning to face your fears, learning to be courageous enough to take calculated risks. Learning to learn from mistakes. Success comes to those who are willing to learn enough about themselves and the work they are involved in to have vision, to pursue that vision. Or simply to be dedicated enough to be the best employee you can be. Sometimes success is simply about deciding to shave rather than go to work with scruff.

This book, *Common Sense Success*, represents most of the stuff you already know about succeeding in life. The problem is we get so busy that we sometimes forget to practice the basics. So think of this book as a refresher course on the fundamentals of success.

I have tried to begin with what I believe to be the foundations for success: desire and dedication. Each successive chapter builds on the ones before, but feel free to poke around the book as the chapter topics interest you. The book can be read from front to back, back to front, or you can start in the middle and flip a coin for your next chapter. I have tried to write the book in a way that makes the chapters easy to access and understand.

To make this book more helpful, I have included a bullet list of main points at the close of each chapter.

More than anything, though, I must tell you another truth about success. In the end none of it matters if you fail in the most important thing in life, which is to come to know why it is you are here looking for success in the first place.

I won't bother you with this right now as I figure you are occuppied with thoughts of business, but I am excited to talk to you more on this if you would like. You can log on to my web site to learn more. Just log on to *www.commonsensesuccess.net* and click *The Most Important Thing* to learn more. I think you already know about this thing too. But this thing, like the rest of life, requires reminding lest a person forget.

One final thing. I love to tell a good story, and in the following pages you can read many exciting and interesting stories. If you have an inspiring or fascinating story of your own that can illustrate a point in one of the chapters I would love to help you share it with our other readers. Just log on to our web site and click *Readers' Stories* and follow the directions on how to include your story on our web site.

Happy and successful reading to you.

My best wishes from my family and friends to yours.

Your friend,

Bill

"Nothing astonishes men so much as common sense and plain dealing."

--Ralph Waldo Emerson

"For any man may be a king in that life in which he is placed if so he may draw forth the sword of success from out of the iron of circumstance."

--Howard Pyle, from *The Story of King Arthur and His Knights*

"We subscribe to the idea that there is no such thing as failure. There's just giving up. We do not give up. We are relentless."

--The Edge, *of the Irish rock band U2*

SECTION ONE
It Takes Dedication

Dedication: Bind yourself to a course of action.

The inukshuk, pronounced "in-ook-shook," is a symbol of someone's dedication to succeed. These stone markers indicate someone has been here before and if you keep going you will find what you desire. In ancient times the dedication to follow these inuksuit (plural, pronounced "in-ook-soo-eet") was a matter of life and death. What the traveler desired was to make it home alive. Success equaled survival. Ancient hunters would dedicate themselves to a path marked by these trustworthy monuments. When they set out to hunt or make the journey home they followed a course of action, and bound themselves to a course of action. Anything less could cost them their life.

CHAPTER ONE

Desire Creates Dedication

Sunday, January 26, 1986. The scene was New Orleans. The event, Super Bowl XX. Thousands of football fans converged in the Louisiana city famed for its jazz to see which football team would walk away with the coveted Vince Lombardi Trophy. Would it be the New England Patriots, a team whose players hadn't recovered from the shock of qualifying for football's ultimate contest after so long a slump? Or would it be the cocky Chicago Bears, the team that had long before recorded and released the popular video *The Super Bowl Shuffle*?

"We don't want to cause no trouble; we just want to do the Super Bowl Shuffle," the team crooned for cameras the day after their only loss of the season. It was a sign that long before even the conference playoffs the Bears had decided this would be their year to walk away with the prize!

The thousands of spectators who traveled to New Orleans to attend the game were not alone in their enthusiasm for the match-up. Millions watched the contest in the comfort of their homes as they tuned-in with a nearly shut-down nation in anticipation of an exciting game. But there was little excitement once the game started. Although the Patriots initially scored three points on a field goal and seven more on a fourth-quarter touchdown, it was the Chicago Bears' show. Quarterback Jim McMahon scored two touchdowns, and three-hundred-pound William "The Refrigerator" Perry rumbled through the Patriots' defense for another.

Unless a person is willing to take meaningful action to turn desires into realities, such desires will remain nothing more than daydreams.

The eighteen points that the two Chicago football stars chalked up would have been more than sufficient to win the game. But, the team racked up another twenty-eight points before the clock ran out to a final score of 46-10. The game was so one-sided that one NBC commentator noted during the third quarter (when the score was 44-3) that "if it were a fight, it would be stopped."

The moral of the story? Success is the result of desire. The Chicago Bears decided early in the season that they were going to win the Super Bowl. They strongly desired to be football's number one team, and it was that desire that made the difference. They decided they were not going to let anything prevent them from making their desire come true.

IT TAKES MORE THAN DESIRE TO SUCCEED

Wouldn't it be nice if desire were all that was required for success? Everyone would enjoy the lifestyle he or she desired. Homelessness would cease to exist. Psychologists and psychiatrists would have to find another line of work because they would have no more patients troubled by unfulfilling, unrewarding lives. Law enforcement agencies would see a sharp reduction in workload because career success would keep most criminals too busy to steal.

> Many people will say they will stay with a new job if they like it. I tell them they will need to learn to like the job if they are going to stay with it.

Unfortunately, the world isn't like that. Desire is to success what bait is to a fisherman; it's critical to the process but it won't eliminate the work required to land the prize. The work is up to the individual, and unless a person is willing to take meaningful action to turn desires into realities, such desires will remain nothing more than daydreams. And daydreams are never as fulfilling as the real thing.

The Chicago Bears had desire for sure. And yes, without this desire they would not have made it to the playoffs. And I am sure they daydreamed about what their success would look like and feel like.

But the Chicago Bears had more than desire going for them. Complimenting this desire was their commitment to do what was necessary to be football's best team for the season. They trained as if their reputations depended upon victory, which in fact it did. Can you imagine the ribbing the team members would have taken had they lost the game or had failed to make even the playoffs? Once "The Super Bowl Shuffle" was released, losing became tantamount to embarrassment.

The Chicago Bears were willing to work for success – something those who fail to succeed are unwilling to do. Many have the desire to succeed but they don't have the willingness to do the uncomfortable things that success often requires.

Success begins with desire and is worked out in dedication.

SOME LIKE IT, SOME DON'T

Of course, you might say that if you were employed at a profession you enjoyed as much as the Bears enjoy football that you would have no trouble dedicating yourself to success. Many people feel that way. In reality many people hold jobs that at best they can take or leave, or at worst they actually despise. I've found over the years that many people will say they will stay with a new job if they like it. I tell them that they'll need to learn to like the job if they're going to stay with it.

Dedication is one of the most misunderstood of all character traits. Many people tend to think that developing dedication to a job depends on whether or not they actually enjoy that task. Without question, enjoyment of the job is a solid plus for the person who seeks to develop dedication, but it certainly isn't a requirement. Many people aren't lucky enough to have jobs they love, but that's no reason for them to throw in the towel and resign themselves to lives of mediocrity.

It isn't necessary to love what you do to be dedicated. It's only necessary that you strongly desire the reward that it will bring.

CHILDREN ARE DEDICATED

To give you an example of dedication, let me tell you about the time my oldest daughter, Jonna, was five years old and wanted a bike. I gave her an old one with training wheels which kept her happy for a while. It wasn't too long before she started to bug me for a bigger bike – one without training wheels. I kept putting her off until, one day, we visited a friend who had a two-wheeler that Jonna wanted to ride.

She asked my permission to ride the bike, which I gave upon one condition: she had to ride it by herself. No one was going to hold her up. I also told her that if she could learn to ride the two-wheeler by herself I would buy her a new bike.

I learned never to issue such challenges to her again without careful consideration. When I checked later to assess her progress I found a bruised, scratched and torn little girl – riding a two-wheeled bicycle like a pro. She taught me a lot about the dedication and reward system. She was willing to persist despite the uncomfortable bumps, bruises and abrasions because there was something in it for her – a new bicycle, which she received.

Dedication – like the dedication my daughter had and the dedication that successful people have in their jobs – grows only out of one thing: desire for the enjoyment the job provides and/or the reward it will bring. Without desire, you will find it difficult if not impossible to dedicate yourself to anything.

WHAT DO YOU NEED?

Desire is the yearning to fill a personal need. If you're hungry you desire food; if you're poor, money. Noted psychologist Dr. Abraham Maslow categorizes human needs into five levels – physical, security, social, ego, and self-fulfillment. Let's explore each one in detail to give you a better idea of what needs you may have. If you feel you lack dedication, reviewing this list may provide the impetus for developing it.

Physical needs.

These are the basics, which include food, clothing and shelter. Until these needs are satisfied, a person usually will not be concerned with higher level needs.

Security needs.

People who satisfy their physical needs generally want to continue to live. Therefore, they seek to fill needs that will ensure a future devoid of despair and/or disaster.

Social acceptance.

No one is an island. All people want acceptance and approval from their peers and, ultimately, to be loved. People need other people to be happy.

Ego gratification.

All of us have the need to be recognized and appreciated for the quality and quantity of our work or hobbies. The person who has satisfied, at least to some extent, the previous three levels will likely devote his or her attention to filling this need.

Self-fulfillment.

The ultimate need is to make a significant contribution to a perceived worthwhile cause, be it charity, your community, state, nation, or the world itself. Jonas Salk undoubtedly achieved self-fulfillment with his polio vaccine; Alexander Graham Bell with the invention of the telephone; and Barack Obama by being elected the nation's 44th president. Of course, self-fulfillment can be obtained without achieving worldwide fame or recognition. It can only be defined by the individual.

WHEN YOU REALLY UNDERSTAND YOUR NEEDS, LIKING YOUR JOB IS A MINOR CONCERN

With the possible exception of physical (survival) needs, all of these needs are subjective in definition. The actions that yield security, social recognition, ego gratification, and self-fulfillment to one person may be regarded as a waste of time and effort to another. To some extent, however, all of us seek to fulfill these needs throughout our lives.

Whether we fulfill them depends on how dedicated we are. For example, if you work for reasons of survival – that is, to eat regularly and pay the rent – then you're filling a need that millions are unable or unwilling to fill for themselves (at least not without some assistance from charity or the government). Therefore, you're dedicated to your survival.

Of course, you can work for reasons other than survival. People who invest their wages for significant returns are dedicated to their future security. They want the peace of mind that comes when a person doesn't have to worry about the next meal.

People can be dedicated to social acceptance. Even if the need for survival and security has been filled, many people work to be contributing members of society. Still others work because of the ego gratification they get by delivering good performances.

Finally, some people work for reasons of self-fulfillment – to make significant work-related contributions to society and/or to obtain sufficient funds that will allow them to enjoy life in the style they desire.

In the end, it all boils down to dedication, doesn't it? If you can't dedicate yourself to your job because you don't like it there are plenty of other reasons to apply yourself with diligence. After all, the need to survive requires just as much – if not more – dedication than the need for self-fulfillment because it offers far less room for failure. Yet think of how much we could achieve if we could learn to dedicate ourselves to the higher areas of human need as much as we dedicate ourselves to survival! With that in mind, it is vital we learn how to dedicate ourselves to all types of jobs to take full advantage of our potential for success.

When you dedicate yourself to that principle, then you will be able to take your best shot at success.

A WORD OF WARNING

You'll notice that I said "take your best shot at success." I did not say that your success would be guaranteed. Nothing can guarantee your success for the same reason you can't possibly control all the factors in your life that might have a bearing on your future.

Let me explain by referring to history again. Two days after the Chicago Bears' Super Bowl triumph, the nation witnessed a grim failure it will never forget.

Tuesday, January 28, 1986. The space shuttle Challenger lifted off from Cape Canaveral with seven astronauts – Challenger commander Francis R. Scobee, pilot Michael J. Smith, mission specialists Dr. Judith A. Resnik, Ellison S. Onizuka and Gregory B. Jarvis; physicist Ronald E. McNair; and volunteer Christa McAuliffe, a school teacher from Concord, New Hampshire, who was to have been the first private citizen in space.

Unfortunately, the flight ended in tragedy. A mechanical malfunction led to the ship's explosion only minutes after lift off, leaving no survivors.

A nation that only two days earlier had witnessed the smashing triumph of the Chicago Bears was now witnessing the worst accident (and failure) in the history of the U.S. space program.

Sometimes the best efforts don't succeed. That's the warning.

The seven astronauts failed in the most tragic sense to achieve success, their lives were lost in the attempt. Though through no faults of their own. All were dedicated to their professions or they never would have been chosen for flight – especially Mrs. McAuliffe, who was selected from a field of 11,000 teachers who applied.

Although her dreams were not realized, she had high hopes, judging from her application letter to NASA. She wrote in her letter, *"I cannot join the space program and restart my life as an astronaut, but this opportunity to connect my abilities as an educator with my interest in history and space is a unique opportunity to fulfill my early fantasies. I watched the space age being born and I would like to participate. My perceptions as a non-astronaut would help complete and humanize the technology of the Space Age. Future historians would use my eyewitness accounts to help in their studies of the impact of the space age on the general population. The chance to share my experiences with educators and to have a direct impact on education is an exciting prospect. The network of national, regional and state educational conferences would make it possible to reach many educators and thereby have a direct impact on students across the United States."*

Clearly, this was Christa McAuliffe's chance to achieve self-fulfillment. Unfortunately, outside forces over which she had absolutely no control prevented her desire from being realized.

The important fact to remember about the Challenger story though is not that there was tragedy, but that Christa McAuliffe (and the other astronauts, of course) were dedicated souls who died trying to achieve personal success. What they undertook to achieve was risky and they knew it. Compare that to a person who dies with a large inventory of untested and unfulfilled dreams. Which person had the better life, regardless of its length? Which person had the better chance of achieving success?

I'm not saying that you should pursue success at the risk of your own life. All I'm saying is that your only chance to succeed depends upon your dedication. If you're dedicated to do the things it will take to be successful, you will be doing your best. Like the Challenger crew, you can't control outside forces that may cause you to fail, but you can try for success.

Yes, the Chicago Bears will always be remembered as winners, but the doomed Challenger crew won't be remembered as losers. Instead, they'll be remembered as dedicated people who lost their lives in an attempt to achieve the highest level of success: self-fulfillment, the highest of human needs.

Win or lose, your only chance of filling your highest needs will depend on the extent of your dedication, which will depend directly upon what you desire out of life.

As I've said before, you can be dedicated to your job without loving it as much as Christa McAuliffe loved the prospect of space travel. It is possible, however, to come to appreciate a seemingly unlovable job through dedication.

Stick with me into the next chapter and I'll explain.

CHAPTER SUMMARY

❖ Success is the result of desire and dedication. Without desire, you will find it difficult, if not impossible, to dedicate yourself to anything.

❖ It isn't necessary to love what you do to be dedicated. It's only necessary that you strongly desire the reward that it will bring.

❖ Desire is the yearning to fill a personal need. Human needs can be classified into five categories – physical, security, social, ego, and self-actualization. Although these needs are very subjective in definition, all of us seek to fulfill these needs throughout our lives.

❖ Your only chance of fulfilling your highest needs will depend on the extent of your dedication, which will depend directly upon what you desire out of life.

❖ Dedication won't guarantee your success, but it will certainly maximize your chances, because the lack of dedication virtually assures failure.

CHAPTER TWO

Dedication Yields Appreciation

I don't think I've ever had a job that I liked at first. Yet, I don't think I've ever had a job that I didn't wind up liking a whole lot, if not actually loving it.

In my life I've picked strawberries (a low-paying job that's terrible on the back and legs), thinned corn (another low-wage, monotonous job with no job advancement opportunity), delivered newspapers (not a job for someone averse to inclement weather and extreme temperatures), pumped gasoline (another job that kept me out in the weather), stocked shelves (a job that kept me indoors), repossessed appliances from defaulting debtors (not the way to get on people's Christmas card lists), and made debt collection calls in the lonely, remote hills of Kentucky (potentially hazardous to the job holder's physical and mental health).

Not one of these jobs was I crazy about, at least at first. But I came to like all of them very much. And it wasn't because I was a glutton for verbal or physical abuse. Instead it was because I enjoyed what my labors yielded.

I enjoyed getting paid and converting the cash into items that I wanted (or needed). For example, when I was in high school and susceptible to peer pressure I felt deficient in the social recognition department because I didn't have a pair of Bass moccasins, which were "the" pair of shoes for teen-agers during this particular period of time.

A pair of Bass moccasins cost $27 back then, which was a lot of money for the time.

Of course, that didn't stop me from wanting them; it only stopped me from buying them – until I saved enough money to get them.

How did I get the money? I picked strawberries, thinned corn, mowed lawns (another job that didn't excite me), stocked shelves and other jobs that I didn't particularly care to make into careers. I dedicated myself to the jobs not because I was a virtuous soul who thrived on hard labor, but because I wanted the Bass moccasins.

WHY PEOPLE ARE DEDICATED

There are lots of reasons why people work. For most it's a way to pay the bills. For some it's an attractive alternative to sitting at home watching daytime game shows and soap operas. Still others work to generate social lives for themselves or because their parents make them in an effort to teach them responsibility. Of course, none of these reasons necessarily lend themselves to dedication. For example, if the person working to survive has sufficient job alternatives available, he or she may only do enough on the job to get by. Dedication has to do with what motivates you the most.

Let's not concern ourselves with the reasons people get their names on other people's payrolls. Instead, let's consider the reasons people dedicate themselves to a job. To my knowledge, there are only four reasons.

To maintain a lifestyle they can't afford to lose.

People can exist on low wages, but if they are used to a certain level of comfort they may not enjoy the downgrading of lifestyles that might result from decreased income. People who depend upon paychecks to maintain their lifestyles – whether the lifestyles are geared toward survival or upper middle class – either are or should be dedicated to their jobs.

Love of job.

Many people dedicate themselves because their careers offer them great satisfaction. That's not to say that these people don't necessarily earn good salaries; it's just that they're more motivated by intrinsic values than they are by cash. The career satisfies these people on at least two levels of needs on Maslow's scale. Aside from survival, the career might satisfy the desires for security, social prestige, ego gratification or self-actualization, if not all of those needs. Of course some people who work for love of career don't receive a great deal of compensation, like many ministers and some artists. Those involved in these latter two professions may be extremely happy with their professions, although they may struggle to make ends meet. As a result, these people may be subject to a great deal of stress caused by financial problems. Not always, but sometimes.

Love of money.

The person who works to produce an income above what is required to maintain a desired lifestyle might be interested in accumulating a significant financial reserve for reasons other than survival. Again, these reasons may include security, social prestige, ego gratification or self-actualization. By the same token, people primarily interested in high salaries sometimes work in careers that provide little or no personal pleasure. It is the promise of earning a lot of cash that is the prime motivation. As a result, these people can be subject to a great deal of stress caused by a dislike for their careers.

All of the above.

This is the desired situation of all who work – to have an enjoyable job that funds a desired lifestyle.

BAD JOBS AREN'T ALL BAD

Bad jobs weren't created to spoil people's lives; they're necessary tasks that need fulfilled. People who offer these jobs are generally averse to doing the work themselves and will gladly pay to have the work done, so there is a lot of opportunity in finding these jobs. Somewhere in my childhood I realized that if I could get a reputation for being a hard worker I could land enough of these jobs to earn money that could be applied to the cause of Bill Arnold and family.

With dedication, we can come to appreciate what we might not ordinarily like. Most of the reasons I've dedicated myself to any job is not because I liked the work as much as I desired the rewards. With each unpleasant job I've ever done I have developed a greater appreciation for dedication. As unpleasant as the experience may have been, the rewards have always been sweet; therefore, it was easier for me to tackle future unpleasant jobs in anticipation of the promised rewards.

The more unpleasant experiences you can undertake and complete to obtain positive results or rewards, the easier it will be in the future to commit yourself to other unpleasant tasks because the rewards will make them worthwhile. Of course, if the rewards aren't sufficient to justify the unpleasant experience, I wouldn't go near the work, and neither should you.

BAD JOBS MAY BE A MATTER OF ATTITUDE

Of course, sometimes, a job or a task is only bad because a person chooses to view it unfavorably. If the person chose to view it in a different light the job or task might not be so bad at all.

Many people say that being a mortician would be a bad job because it involves working with dead people and their grieving survivors. Yet, morticians view themselves as counselors who help bereaved people deal positively with their sorrow while providing a dignified disposition of the dead. That certainly sounds honorable to me.

In fact, I hold what many people consider to be a bad job. Debt collectors have been vilified throughout the ages. Many people say they don't know whether debt collectors are a cut above or a cut below IRS agents and used car salespeople. Yet, if it weren't for successful debt collection efforts, credit as we know it would cease to exist because merchants couldn't afford to absorb the massive losses that otherwise would result. Therefore, I choose to view myself as not only a guardian of the nation's credit system, but also as a counselor who helps individuals protect their own credit ratings by encouraging them to pay past due accounts.

If you enjoy the rewards that your job yields, but not the job itself, perhaps you could learn to enjoy your career by altering your attitude. If this sounds like too large of an order to carry out, or if you'd prefer a better job altogether, sufficient dedication and successful execution of the "bad" job or task may eliminate the need for you to continue it.

Some employers subscribe to the school of thought that a person who can do a bad job well will perform remarkably with a good one.

If you perform a job competently and enthusiastically you may be offered a better one either by your own employer or another. Some employers subscribe to the school of thought that a person who can do a bad job well will perform remarkably with a good one. Many times this is true.

Let me tell you about Don Shearer, an employee of American Accounts whom I hired several years ago prior to selling the business. Previously he had worked as a meat cutter for a local grocery – not a bad job at all, although some people might not agree.

However, Don decided he didn't want to make a career out of cutting meat so he came to work for us at the age of 21 as a debt collector. Again, considering the unpopular image of debt collectors, many people might think that Don traded one bad job for another. Don didn't think so.

Through dedication Don became a $40,000-per-month collector at a time when $25,000 per month was considered great. He became a manager of five collectors within a year. Six months later, he became a department manager, then a collections manager who supervised 70 to 80 collectors.

Do you think Don dedicated himself because he loved the job of collecting debts? I don't think so. Of course he might in fact love the job, but I think he dedicated himself because he wanted a new home and a new Corvette, both of which he now owns. If for no other reason I suspect Don is dedicated to his job because he doesn't want to be a meat-cutter again. Considering his performance and his dedication, I believe the only meat he'll ever again cut will be what he eats.

It all boils down to dedication. The person who is dedicated will learn to enjoy his or her "bad" job, or eventually will achieve a more favorable position, simply because of his or her dedication to performing a given task well.

On the other hand, the person who isn't dedicated to the competent execution of his or her job or task is likely doomed to be saddled with it forever – or at least until there is a change of attitude.

THE ENEMY OF DEDICATION

If dedication is so powerful that it can make you appreciate unpleasant tasks, why do many studies indicate that a majority of North American workers are at least unhappy with their careers, and some of them actually despise them? The answer is simple – they're not dedicated.

Why they are not dedicated is unimportant. To list every individual reason would be a massive task indeed. To simplify matters considerably, many of these people are guilty of embracing the enemy of dedication: rationalization

You can't be dedicated to anything if you can think of a reason why you shouldn't be dedicated. For example, many people make up their minds that they aren't going to be dedicated to their jobs because they feel they aren't paid what they are worth. Of course, some people should be glad they aren't paid what they are worth; if they were, their salary would be cut.

Of course, reasons for not being dedicated vary. Many people aren't dedicated because they don't like their supervisors, or their working conditions, or their co-workers, or company policy, or third shift, or second shift, or first shift.

Rationalization ... Nothing more than making yourself feel good about something you will likely regret later.

Because they're unhappy they decide that the effort they expend will be limited only to what is necessary to "get by." They won't make the extra effort to improve their salaries or their job situations, because they've decided to take the easy way out.

This is called rationalization, which is nothing more than making yourself feel good about doing something that you'll likely regret later.

As a result, the discontented worker will likely remain the discontented worker because he or she never takes positive action to improve or change his or her job situation. Instead, the worker finds justification not to do what is necessary to lead to an upgraded career situation.

Anytime you allow rationalization to stand in the way of dedication, you'll develop a conflict. The two mix like oil and water. It's like trying to reach a point north by heading south. It never works, ever.

There is simply no substitute for dedication! There's only one way to develop it, and that's by clearly defining the reward you stand to gain be it material or intrinsic – for accomplishment of the task or job.

DEDICATION CANNOT BE TAUGHT

Remember, the dedication you develop will depend on the intensity of your desire. It's certainly something that cannot be taught. No matter how much you may want your children to save money for their futures, they won't save until it suits them. They've got to want to be dedicated; you won't teach it to them.

Teaching someone dedication is like trying to teach a pig to sing; it doesn't work, and it annoys the pig. You've got to want to develop dedication before you can develop it.

Let me give you a tip: You can develop the dedication to your given job or task provided you are willing to endure the discomfort it takes to achieve the desired results.

Let me tell you about some people – some of whom I know and others of whom I've read about – who knew what they wanted and developed the dedication to get it because they were willing to endure discomfort.

John Goddard

I met this man more than twenty years ago, but I had read about him many times before then. John Goddard is an inspirational person who has had a profound effect on my life, and so many other lives. He is an adventurer and innovator whose achievements have led to his being a role model for thousands of people throughout the past four decades.

At the age of 15 Goddard put down on paper 127 desires he wanted to fulfill in his lifetime. It was an extraordinary ambition. His list included a desire to journey to the ends of the earth and beyond. The list included a mix of wild adventure and peculiar desires.

By the time I had met him at the age of 62, he had accomplished most of them.

Some of his accomplishments include: exploring the Nile, Amazon, Congo and Colorado rivers; studying primitive cultures in the Congo, New Guinea, Brazil, Borneo and the Sudan (where he was nearly buried alive in a sandstorm); climbing a dozen major mountains, including Mount Fuji, the Matterhorn and Mt. Kilimanjaro; learning to fly a plane; underwater exploration of the sea; writing a book; circumnavigating the globe; marrying and having children (he's had five) and dozens of other accomplishments that many people never dare to consider. On his list of unfulfilled desires, he wants to visit the moon.

> "I met so many adults who felt they had missed the boat in life. It kind of scared me into action. I thought, I don't want to wake up some morning middle-aged, feeling I had kinda wasted life..."
>
> --John Goddard

How did Goddard develop the desire to accomplish these feats? "Thank God there was no TV when I was growing up," he told me during a telephone conversation. "I think that was important because I manufactured my own recreation and interests."

And what made him dedicated to do this? "I met so many adults who felt they missed the boat in life. It kind of scared me into action. I thought, 'I don't want to wake up some morning middle-aged, feeling I had kind of wasted life and I hadn't done the things I really wanted.'"

"Unfortunately, we live in a world of mediocrity, where most people are content with the status quo and just to drift along, each day a carbon copy of the day before. But every once in a while, they'll be touched by someone who is a live wire, and it can really open them up."

"The only reason I ever submit to interviews is maybe the fact that they can lift up someone, encourage them ... I never have been comfortable talking about my own achievements because I think they're only important to me and my family. But every once in while, I'll have someone who tells me that I got them off drugs, or encouraged them to go on and finish college, and that's tremendously worthwhile to me."

John Goddard endured many discomforts, but he brought his dreams to reality through dedication. And so can you. And in so doing, you too can inspire others.

As of 2009, John had successfully achieved 109 of his 127 goals, lacking the climbing of Mt. Everest, appearing in a Tarzan movie, and owning a cheetah, among a few other adventures.

Roger Reynolds

In 1974, as a 21-year-old man he was a member of the U.S. Army's Golden Knights, a 27-member skydiving team. During a performance in Charlottesville, Virginia, Reynold's main and auxiliary chutes failed to open properly and he plunged unimpeded, striking the ground at an estimated speed of 80 mph. Most bones in his body were shattered and doctors offered no encouragement for his survival. But he did survive and doctors credited his determination with pulling him through. After spending 14 months in a body cast he was warned by his physicians that he would forever walk with a limp and that he would never run again. That thought didn't sit well with Reynolds who then developed the determination to prove his doctors wrong. And he did. Through determined (though extremely painful) practice, the limp disappeared and Reynolds slowly but surely developed the ability to run again. In November 1983 he successfully completed a full marathon in Bloomington, Indiana.

Lane Bryant

Widowed and virtually destitute and mother of a six-month-old son at the age of 21, this young woman was dedicated to the survival of her child and herself. Pawning her diamond earrings in 1899, she purchased a sewing machine and made clothes for women. From these humble beginnings arose a clothing business for pregnant and large-proportioned women that was valued at $50 million at the time of her death.

All of these people had to endure varying degrees of discomfort to succeed, and all of these people were dedicated for their own reasons. Of course, these reasons can be viewed from either a positive or negative viewpoint.

Positively speaking, John Goddard wanted to be an adventurer, Roger Reynolds wanted to run again, and Lane Bryant wanted her son and herself to survive.

But on the other hand the reasons for dedication also can be viewed from a negative viewpoint. Sometimes negative reasons can be great incentives too. John Goddard didn't want to be like the adults he had known who had "missed the boat" and, thus, were living lives of mediocrity; Roger Reynolds didn't want to walk with a limp, his athletic life to be history; and Lane Bryant didn't want to beg for support.

These people developed dedication not only for love of rewards but out of fear of the alternatives. Each person knew exactly what he or she wanted to achieve.

How about you? Will rewards motivate you to be dedicated? If not, will fear of the alternative sufficiently inspire you? If you don't want to experience the results of inaction and a lack of dedication, then you had better develop some exciting desires that you would like to bring to reality.

These are called goals, and that's the subject of the next chapter. Read on and I'll help you establish goals that will add meaning and purpose to your life.

CHAPTER SUMMARY

❖ There are only four reasons why people dedicate themselves to a job – to maintain a lifestyle they can't afford to lose, love of job, acquisition of wealth or a combination of the previous three reasons. The last reason clearly is the ideal job situation.

❖ Through dedication to achieving promised rewards, it is possible to appreciate a job that you normally might not like.

❖ Sometimes, a bad job may be only a matter of a bad attitude. With a different attitude, you might come to appreciate the job, or at least be performing it well enough to be offered a better job.

❖ Rationalization is the enemy of dedication. You can't be dedicated to anything if you can think of a reason not to be.

❖ Dedication to a job or task can be developed by enduring the discomfort that the job or task involves.

CHAPTER THREE

Achievers Take All

I once read that the human race can be divided into four categories – survivors, takers, winners and achievers. In which group would you rank yourself?

The article stated that 60 percent of us are survivors. These are people who work regularly to earn money to support themselves. Like all of us, they'll be hit with unexpected expenses and circumstances periodically that will try them. But don't worry about them; they'll survive, because they're survivors. They won't lie down and die just because life gets tough.

This is certainly an admirable quality, and it's encouraging to know that six out of every 10 people are survivors.

Unfortunately, survivors merely survive. When life is sailing smoothly they tend to go along for the ride. Rather than concentrating on how to improve the quality of their lives they generally and readily accept the status quo as long as it accepts them. If there are no pressing problems to threaten their peaceful existence they fall into a routine. They tend not to take the initiative to improve the quality of their careers or lifestyles; instead they reserve their extraordinary efforts for the task of survival. As a result they get by.

Survivors react, takers manipulate and winners work diligently to fulfill others' plans. Achievers make their own plans and work to see the plans succeed.

True, survivors are better than takers, which make up 27 percent of the population. Roughly one out of every four people is a taker. Though far fewer than survivors, the ranks of takers are sadly significant.

Prisons are full of takers and the free world has no shortage of them. All they want in life is their "fair share" and part of everybody else's. Give them inches and they'll take miles. Ask not what they can do for you; instead, ask what you can do for them. As they see it, the world owes them a living.

No matter what happens a taker isn't to blame. All of his or her many problems can be blamed on a domineering mother, or a frequently absent father, or the fact that he or she was an oldest child, a middle child, a youngest child or an only child. Takers always have someone or something to blame, other than themselves. When life dumps problems on them (which happens often with takers), they do their level best (through the power of guilt) to see that someone else shares, if not totally accepts, the responsibility of solving it.

This philosophy is quite normal for people under the age of six. All people are born takers. Unfortunately one out of every four never stops. As a result they get lonely ... and often bitter.

Fortunately taking isn't a terminal condition. With concerted effort and a change of attitude a taker can become a survivor, a winner or even an achiever. Unfortunately many of them never stop taking long enough to try to become anything else

On the brighter side, one out of every 10 people is a winner. These are admirable people indeed. They have winning attitudes. When faced with problems they solve them. When presented with tasks they complete them. They're good workers and are real assets to anyone lucky enough to employ them. As a result they get ahead ... but still not as far as they could.

You've probably heard it said that in a poker game or prizefight the "winner takes all." But even winners don't get it all. In the game of life "all" is reserved for the achievers.

Achievers are the 3 percent of the people who take the time to plan their lives and then work to bring their plans to reality. Rather than waiting for life to hand them an opportunity to succeed, they make their own. While they don't relish problems, they welcome problems for the opportunities they provide because they know that problems are nothing more than opportunities in disguise. As a result, they get what they want ... and sometimes more. What makes the difference? Simply stated, it boils down to planning.

Survivors don't plan; they react. Takers don't plan; they manipulate. Even winners don't plan; if they did, they'd be achievers. Instead, winners work diligently and constructively toward someone else's plan, and they're rewarded for their efforts.

But achievers are winners who plan and are willing to work on their own plans just as diligently as they would those of others. They don't need the incentive of immediate compensation to motivate them; they're willing to endure long hours of work with little or no immediate reward to bring their plans to reality.

Achievers set goals, and then they go for them. As a result, they are the "winners" who take all.

GO WITH GOALS

Goal setting is nothing more than planning for success. If you fail to plan for success you will successfully plan to fail. It's that simple.

Of course when you set a goal you must also establish a plan that will bring your goal to reality. It isn't enough simply to want to achieve your goal. As Dale Carnegie said, *"You can't get anywhere in this world wanting to do it."* Planning is vitally essential to the goal-setting process.

Planning to succeed in life is similar to taking an automobile trip to an unfamiliar location. Your destination is your goal, the road map is your plan. Follow it and you'll get to where you want to go. If you ignore it you'll never find your destination because you won't know what route to take.

Goals are to people what a rudder is to a ship. A ship will go in circles without a rudder; people will do much the same without goals.

Goals are blueprints to success. The successful person lives by them for all facets of life – physical, mental, spiritual, career, financial, social and family. They are what separates the achievers from the rest of the population. People with goals are like builders with good building plans. A person going through life without goals is like a building contractor going through the work week without building plans. The building contractor would just be stumbling and guessing their way through the building process.

CHILLING STATISTICS

Do you know that out of every 100 retired people only three are self-sufficient? The other 97 must depend upon government support to survive!

It has also been said that only 4 to 5 percent of Americans set goals, and that less than 5 percent of all American households operate on budgets.

I think these statistics speak for themselves. Success requires planning. The person who isn't willing to plan isn't willing to succeed. Yet few people appreciate the benefits of wise planning until it's too late.

> They were good planners when it came to aquiring short-term pleasures. But when it came to plannning long-term security at the expense of short-term pleasure they couldn't be bothered.

It's not that these people didn't know how to plan. In fact, many of them were good at planning. They invested countless hours of planning to achieve vacation goals. They planned their finances to accommodate the purchase of airline tickets, new clothes and souvenirs. They were good planners when it came to acquiring short-term pleasures; but when it came to planning for long-term security at the expense of short-term pleasure they couldn't be bothered.

Of course, when they reached old age they became bitter because they had neither security nor pleasure. A life sentence to poverty is not a good way to end life. Yet, think how they would have succeeded in life if they had applied their planning expertise to worthwhile goals.

IMPROVE YOUR LIFE WITH GOALS

Don't wait until it's too late. You can change your life by setting goals. So to maximize your chances of setting goals that you will be able to achieve, let's talk about the characteristics of successful goals.

Successful goals are specific.

After I founded my business, American Accounts Collection Agency, Inc., one of the first problems I encountered arose from setting vague goals. Whenever I was asked how much money I wanted to collect the first year, I'd reply by saying, "All that I can." When asked how much profit I wanted the business to make the first year, I'd say, "All it can."

When you set vague goals you are running a race without a finish line; you must keep running to stay ahead. This can quickly lead to burnout because there is no point in time when you can relax and celebrate. Vague goals don't define success. By the same token they don't define failure either. If my business had collected less than a satisfactory amount of money I had a built-in escape valve. I could have said, "Well, that's all the business was able to collect, so it reached its goal."

The saddest people in life are those who always and only want more. Unfortunately they never get enough. But it's still a crying shame when people allow themselves to settle for far less than they could have received if they had planned properly.

It didn't take me long to realize that I needed some specific goals. For example, collecting X amount of dollars became a one-year goal – the minimum I would accept as satisfactory. Then I set a "stretch" goal of X + Y amount of dollars. If I reached that, it was time to celebrate. And, of course, anything above X + Y was pure gravy.

When you set goals I suggest you take the same approach. Establish a minimum acceptable goal and then set a "stretch" goal for additional motivation. This will tend to ensure that you will give your very best effort and increase your chances of reaching your minimum.

Successful goals are measurable.

Meaningful goals require measurable limits. For example, to finish a long-distance race isn't a challenging goal if you have all day to devote to the race; you can alter your pace – even stop running altogether – to suit yourself and still finish the race ... if you don't mind finishing last. With no time limit on the race you'll lack sufficient motivation to give it your best shot.

On the other hand, finishing a race like, say, an 8-mile run, within 64 minutes is a measurable goal. In fact, it's one I set for myself several years ago. Did I achieve my goal? Not quite – I missed it by three minutes, completing the run within 67 minutes. Next time, however, I'll make it. (Just because you fail to achieve a goal doesn't mean you can't try again!)

Successful goals are attainable.

While failure to set a measurable time frame results in a lack of motivation, don't be afraid to allow yourself a reasonable amount of time to achieve your goals. Goals must be attainable or the pursuit of them will be nothing more than exercise in futility.

In 1985 American Accounts Collection Agency listed $100,000,000 in accounts to collect. It took 16 years of hard work to generate this amount of business. If I had set $100,000,000 as my first-year quota I would have fallen sadly short and possibly would have become seriously discouraged.

When people fail to reach goals, many times it's because they try to achieve them too quickly. Any meaningful success requires time; don't be afraid to allot sufficient time to reach your goal.

Successful goals are relevant.

Goals must be relevant to your overall purpose. For example, when I'm at work I'm not going to be planning my weekend activities; on the other hand when I'm at church God gets my attention, not my business.

Take the race I ran, for instance. I set a 64-minute goal, allowing eight minutes per mile. I did not set a 40-minute goal, which would allow only five minutes per mile. Why? I just want to stay in shape; it's not my desire to become a professional distance runner.

Life is multi-faceted; the best success is reserved for those who work toward achieving relevant goals. People who try to be the best at everything they do generally end up frustrated by failure.

Successful goals are time bound.

Goals must be classified into their proper categories, short-range, intermediate or long-range.

For example, if you're 20 years away from retirement and your long-range goal is to retire with a net worth of $500,000, then a short range goal may be to acquire a certain amount of cash within three to five years, and an intermediate goal might be a greater amount still in a decade.

A person who sets a time-bound goal starts at the end point and works backwards to the present. If the goal is to lose 24 pounds within six months, an intermediate goal might be to lose 12 pounds within three months, or four pounds per month. This means that a short-range goal would be to lose about a pound per week. That's an attainable figure since health experts say that a person should lose no more than 1 to 2 percent of his or her weight per week.

SMART goals: Specific, Measurable, Attainable, Relevant, Time-bound.

For life in general, short-range goals generally run from six months to a year in duration, intermediate goals run from three to five years and long-range goals are 10 years or more away. It's all a matter of perspective, which is very important to the goal setting process.

Make sure that all of your goals include these characteristics – specific, measurable, attainable, relevant and time bound. Take the first letter of each characteristic and you have the word "smart." If your goals are "smart," you'll have clear-cut, meaningful goals to pursue and your life will have solid direction.

ALL KINDS OF GOALS

Of course, when you start setting goals make sure that you cover your entire life. Of what value is career success if your family life is a disaster? What good is financial success if you lose your physical and/or mental health in the process?

True success is not one-dimensional, it's the total picture. It's absolutely worthless unless it can be shared with loved ones. Charles Dickens' Ebeneezer Scrooge in *A Christmas Carol* is a classic example of a man who allowed his one-dimensional success to make him miserable. Of course by the story's end Scrooge had learned his lesson and in the process discovered the true meaning of success.

Let's review the areas of life in which you may want to set goals to ensure that your success is truly multi-dimensional.

Set spiritual goals.

This is where it all starts. You owe your existence to God. He has put you here for a purpose and it's your responsibility to discover what this purpose is. I am not saying for you to go out and discover a religion. I am saying for you to discover what underlies it all. If you don't have a reason why you wake up each day then ultimately you are just wandering through life blind. Spiritual goals are the underlying goals that motivate everything you do in life. So it is best if you think about these things and set some goals in this underlying part of your life.

Set family goals.

Watch this one carefully. Since you see your family every day it's easy to take them for granted. The best way to avoid this is by setting goals to enjoy time with your family. If you're married pay special attention to your spouse if you want him or her to pay special attention to you. Divorce courts are filled with people who have learned that good spouses are hard to find.

I like to take my family on exciting trips throughout the United States and the world. We have a goal to travel to all fifty states and the world's major countries. Through the enjoyment of these experiences they can learn first-hand about the dedication and reward system.

Set career goals.

We've already covered the finer points of dedication to career, whether or not you actually enjoy the work. Set career goals to make the most of your employment; such goals can only work to your benefit.

Set physical health goals.

A premature death can ruin any kind of other success you might enjoy. I say this with a bit of humor, but it is true. What good is your life if it ends early? Worse, what good is your life if your lack of physical care leads to a preventable disability? Stay in good shape through proper diet and regular exercise. Just three times per week of moderate to vigorous exercise can keep your body operating at peak efficiency.

Set mental health goals.

Devote time to your mind. A healthy body can allow you to live a long time, and a healthy mind can have a positive impact on the quality of the life you live.

Set financial goals.

Remember the 94 percent of the retired people who

regularly need helping hands for the rest of their lives – don't be one of them. Set short-range, intermediate and long-term financial goals to provide for your future. Do not overlook or underestimate the significance of this area, because poverty has a way of adversely affecting all of life's other facets.

Recreation.

Everybody needs an occasional break from routine, whether it is a game of racquetball or an extended vacation. Make sure you get enough of these breaks by setting recreational goals.

Charity.

The only way to make sure that we have it all is by giving to others who are in need. This can take the form of contributions (financial or otherwise) to charities, communities or whole countries. Sam Walton established a $3.6 million scholarship for students of Latin American countries to attend Harding University, a Christian school operated by the Churches of Christ in Searcy, Arkansas. Scholarship winners are brought to the United States where they learn about capitalism and the American way of life. Walton hoped they would return home to introduce our way of life to their communities.

Contribute to your total success by setting goals in each and every one of these areas. You'll find the rewards of multi-dimensional success to be pleasing, indeed.

Of course if your goal is worth pursuing at all then you should do your best to achieve it. Otherwise you'll be short-changing yourself.

So make sure that the goal you set is worthwhile, that it

is consistent with the way you see yourself and the way you would want others you value to see you, including God.

But most of all, make sure the goal is something that you truly want to achieve. It makes no difference how much anyone else would like for you to achieve the goal; if it's not your desire, you probably won't achieve it and most definitely wouldn't enjoy it even if you did.

But if your goal is consistent with your values and desires, your chance of success will be good, provided you give your all to your goal.

The next chapter will discuss in detail just what you must do to bring your goals to reality. It also discusses the necessity of sacrifice. In virtually every case, attaining a goal depends on the sacrifice of something you already have. Read on and I'll explain just how sacrifice can work for you.

CHAPTER SUMMARY

❖ Goal setting is nothing more than planning for success. If you fail to plan for success, you will, in effect, successfully plan to fail.

❖ Successful goals are specific, measurable, attainable, relevant, and time bound. If your goals are "smart," you'll have clear-cut, meaningful goals to pursue, and your life will have solid direction.

❖ Various goals should be set to increase your chances of achieving multidimensional success. When setting goals, keep in mind your wants and needs relating to your spirituality, family, career, physical health, mental health, financial status, recreational pursuits and favorite charitable causes.

CHAPTER FOUR

Make Goals Worth Your Effort

The scene was Chicago; the era was Prohibition. Two shotgun blasts sounded the funeral knell for an associate of crime czar Al Capone known as "Artful Eddie." He wasn't the first Chicago mobster to be rubbed out by Capone's gang for squealing, and he certainly wouldn't be the last. His violent death would serve as an example to anyone foolish enough to believe that he could "rat" on Capone and live to talk about it.

Yet, "Artful Eddie" was no fool. A skilled lawyer by profession, he had won his own acquittal in 1923 on an illegal booze indictment. Later he and Capone joined forces to form a lucrative dog track management syndicate that spanned the nation. Yes, "Artful Eddie" was nobody's fool.

So why did he inform on the mob? Such an action carried a high price tag and Eddie definitely knew he'd have to pick up the tab. When a Capone gang member squealed, past personal friendships didn't count; the penalty was swift and violent death. This was a non-negotiable condition, as many of Capone's ex-associates and their survivors had already learned – the hard way.

> To achieve or acquire something you don't have, you're going to have to sacrifice something you've already got.

There must have been something in it for Eddie to "sing" to authorities, but it certainly wasn't money. The dog tracks had made Eddie an extremely wealthy man. It wasn't revenge, because Capone hadn't double-crossed him.

Eddie's reason for selling out his unsavory associates ran deeper than financial gain or revenge. It was an act of love. His son, Butch, mattered more to him than money, power, prestige ... even more than life itself. And Eddie proved that by talking.

In return for his information, the underworld stigma was lifted from the family name. Son Butch was later accepted by the U.S. Naval Academy and subsequently joined the U.S. Navy as a fighter pilot. On February 20, 1942, he shot six Japanese bombers out of the sky in combat over the Pacific. For that, he became the first naval aviator of World War II to be personally awarded the Congressional Medal of Honor.

Unfortunately, a year later Butch was killed in aerial combat. In memory, the people of Chicago paid tribute to Lt.

Commander Edward Henry 'Butch' O'Hare by naming an airport after him – O'Hare International Airport, which is now one of the busiest commercial airports in the world.

Edward J. "Artful Eddie" O'Hare had a goal – to eliminate any obstacle that might prevent his son from living a meaningful, productive life. To achieve that goal, "Artful Eddie" was willing to sacrifice his very life – and he did.

GOALS REQUIRE SACRIFICE

This story illustrates the necessity of sacrifice to achieve a goal. You see, to achieve or acquire something you don't have, you're going to have to sacrifice something you've already got.

I hope you won't have to sacrifice your life to achieve your goals, but I also hope that you won't mind sacrificing anything that might prevent you from achieving them.

I know of no significant goal that doesn't require sacrifice. Most achievement goals require the sacrifice of leisure time at the very least: some even require the sacrifice of money to be invested in education or other forms of self-improvement. Acquisition goals generally require at least the sacrifice of money and, in some cases, a degree of free time to be devoted to efforts to raise additional funds, such as a part-time job or extra hours on a regular job. Health goals generally require sacrifice of some kind. An overweight person must sacrifice sweets and desserts for a successful diet and free time for exercise: an addict who seeks to recover must sacrifice whatever it is to which he or she is addicted, be it caffeine, nicotine, alcohol, or narcotics.

Dedication too often is seen in terms of what must be sacrificed rather than what will be gained. Assuming that the goal is worth more to the goal-setter than what must be given up to achieve it, the sacrifice is merely the price to pay for achieving the goal.

JAPAN HAD TO SACRIFICE, BUT IT PAID OFF

There is no free lunch in life. Anything significant is going to cost something. For example, two years after the death of Lieutenant Commander O'Hare, President Harry S. Truman authorized the dropping of the atomic bombs on the Japanese cities of Hiroshima and Nagasaki, bringing an end to the Japanese involvement in World War II, and many thought at the time this might also end the Japanese nation.

Nearly seventy years later, this country that's about the size of the state of California, has become a leader in the world's steel industry, practically taken over the electronics industry and has given U.S. automakers a serious run for their money. In fact, it only took a couple of decades for this tiny island nation to rebuild and dominate the world in steel production and other industries. Today, Japan is one of the world's largest economies.

This admirable achievement was brought about by synergism – the combined action of several agents to produce an effect greater than the sum of their individual effects. In short, the Japanese people sacrificed individual gain to achieve the accelerated economic growth of their country. At the end of World War II the Japanese people faced the mammoth task of rebuilding a war-torn nation: they responded by setting a mammoth-sized goal and pursuing it with extreme dedication and sacrifice. As history will attest, it paid off in a big way.

For example, Japan has one of the lowest mortality rates and the highest life spans of any country. The country is one of the world's top economic powers. It has one of the highest literacy percentages, one of the the highest levels of education, and five times the number of patent applications on file than the United States. Japan also has one of the world's largest cities, Tokyo, which has one of the world's lowest crime rates.

WHAT STANDS IN YOUR WAY?

The Japanese people donn't stop working after putting in eight hours per day; the average workweek in Japan is 60 hours. They didn't let their desires for leisure interfere with the country's goal. They also didn't reward themselves by frittering away their salaries. Quite the contrary, Japanese people save 20 percent of their disposal income.

The Japanese are highly dedicated people and very accountable to their companies. As an example, the president of Japan Air Lines offered his resignation the day after a company flight crashed, killing hundreds of people. The official had absolutely nothing to do with the crash and no one had even suggested that he had been negligent in any way. "But the accident happened," Yasumoto Takagi said in his resignation letter to Prime Minister Yasuhiro Nakasone, "and I have to take responsibility for it."

During a visit to Japan several years ago I learned why the Japanese people have become so successful. They have an expression, "hara wo kokuru." It means that a person is resolved to succeed – whatever the outcome. No doubt this expression was the motto of many young Japanese pilots who flew "kamikaze" missions during World War II. These young pilots purposely crashed their planes into U.S. battleships, causing serious damage to the vessels, if not outright destroying them. Of course, these pilots would forfeit their lives in the process, but their objective would be achieved. This is another case of a goal that required the sacrifice of a life.

The Japanese are very dedicated people because they try to keep their eyes on their goals. As a result, they are not tempted or plagued with obstacles that beset so may others in the world.

WATCH OUT FOR OBSTACLES!

I watched a football game some years ago between the Indianapolis Colts and the San Diego Chargers. A Colts quarterback threw the ball long and hard down field to a wide receiver. The receiver, who was the subject of hot pursuit from a San Diego team member, looked back to see how close his pursuer was. In so doing he took his eye off the ball and, of course, missed the catch.

If you're running to win, you're concerned with results; if you're running to keep from losing, you're primarily concerned with obstacles.

Immediately I was reminded of what happens to people when they take their eyes off their goals: they often don't reach them because they're sidetracked by obstacles.

In races, the fastest runners always look ahead; they're not worried about who is behind them. They know if they turn to look back they run the risk of losing the advantage. They know that when you run to win, you run a lot faster than when you're running to keep from losing. If you're running to win you're concerned with results; if you're running to keep from losing, you're primarily concerned with obstacles.

Obstacles are what you see when you take your eyes off your goal. To a dieter with an eye on a trim figure, an obstacle is a piece of pie that looks too good to pass up. To an addict with an eye on an addiction-free existence, an obstacle is whatever it is he or she is trying to give up. To an achiever, an obstacle is anything that would entice him or her to be idle.

The best way to avoid obstacles is to keep your eye on your goal. For the many courageous Japanese who sacrifice for a 60-hour work week, the reward is the national pride and work ethic. The obstacle could be the long hours. Often the obstacle gets more attention than the goal itself. When you're in danger of being derailed, stay on course by keeping your eye on the goal.

SET BIG GOALS

It is vital to set goals to develop the incentive to achieve and, thus, live a meaningful life. So if you must set goals, it is wise to set big goals. Average goals may be relatively easy to obtain, but the achievement of average goals won't distinguish you from the mass of people. After all, average is just as close to failing as succeeding.

So break out of the average mold to achieve above-average results! There is no better way to exceed average limitations than by acquiring above average motivation. This is done only by setting above-average goals.

The three biggest goals I've ever set – and accomplished – also have been the most rewarding. The first goal was establishing American Accounts Collection Agency, Inc., in 1970. What I really desired was independence; I never again wanted to be dependent upon someone else for a job. The prospect of self-employment and independence gave me the incentive to start my business.

Let me tell you, it was anything but easy. First, I quit my job with a finance company and sold my car for business start-up funding. In trying to acquire past-due accounts to use as seeds to start the agency I met with rejection upon rejection. I contacted twenty to thirty companies per day and asked them to place their old accounts with my collection agency; most of them didn't give me the time of day. In fact it took 18 months of calls and rejections before I finally was authorized to list accounts for my first hospital client.

I was very discouraged until someone told me that I would go broke if I went into business for myself. I'm not the kind of guy that should be told that I can't do something unless the person telling me so actually wants to watch me succeed. That warning helped me become even more dedicated to my goal because I wanted to prove this person wrong. Of course, I did. I finally landed 35 "difficult to collect" accounts, so termed by the agency from which I obtained them. That description wasn't wrong, either. Collecting on those accounts also was difficult but I succeeded. When I saw that my business was destined for success I got a natural high (I'm not interested in any other kind) that's simply indescribable.

My second toughest goal was balancing my family life and my career. Starting your own business requires an inordinate amount of time and energy. I was willing to pay the price – to a point, that is. I didn't mind the work involved but when I realized that my dedication to business was being developed at the expense of my family I realized that the price was too high. I had to strike a balance with which I could live both in my career and at home.

That wasn't easy. I love my family and I could spend 24 hours per day with them. On the other hand I love my job and could spend 24 hours per day with it. It doesn't take a mathematician to determine this could be an unsolvable equation.

I set a goal of striking a harmonious balance and I achieved it. Career is very important, but I shudder to think what might have occurred had I placed a greater value on it than I did my family. Success is nothing without loved ones with which to share it.

In addition to devoting one night each week to my family and various other nights to individual family members, I also set a goal to travel to all the countries of the world and take my family with me.

The third toughest goal I ever set was controlling my diet. Several years ago I weighed 198 pounds, which were distributed on my 5-foot 7-inch frame. On my feet I looked like a walking basketball. On the seashore I looked like a beached whale.

Now I maintain a weight of 155 pounds, seven pounds less than I did when I was discharged from the service in 1966. I avoided obstacles while dieting by keeping my eye on my goal of weighing 155 pounds. Now that I've achieved it I will indulge in desserts and occasional sweets, but I do so in moderation, which I find much more enjoyable than abstinence.

My point is, I could have settled for average goals. Instead of forming my own business I could have settled for increased income from my previous job at the finance company. Instead of striking a real balance between career and family I could have settled for occasional token appearances at home. Instead of losing more than 40 pounds I could have settled for losing 10 or even 20. However, had I settled for average goals I would have had to settle for average results, and average results wouldn't have solved my above-average problems.

Let me bring up Don Shearer again. He was the dedicated American Accounts employee I mentioned in a previous chapter who wanted more out of life than a meat cutter's salary could provide. He developed above average dedication by setting and achieving above-average goals. After superb performances as a collector, manager and department head, he set a goal of becoming a vice president of the company, a goal which he achieved.

Strive for excellence. When you set big goals you have the potential to enjoy equally big rewards. More importantly, you'll develop the dedication to persist in the pursuit of the goals. This means that you'll have the satisfaction of living life to the fullest while you strive for success. That's what life is all about, isn't it?

PERSISTENCE IS ESSENTIAL

Achieving my big goals was not easy for me, and achieving yours won't be easy for you. There probably will be times that you'll be tempted to quit.

I can't promise you that persistence will result in the achievement of your goal any more than NASA could promise every flight would be perfect. I can, however, promise that if you quit your goal definitely won't be reached. Therefore, persistence is the best thing you'll have going for you.

President Calvin Coolidge put a great deal of stock into persistence. He offered these words on the subject: "*Nothing in the world can take the place of persistence. Talent will not; nothing is more common than unsuccessful men with talent. Genius will not; unrewarded genius is almost a proverb. Education will not; the world is full of educated derelicts. Persistence and determination alone are omnipotent.*"

Let me tell you about a fellow who was persistent. In 1960, Thomas S. Monaghan, at the age of 23, went into business for himself in Ypsilanti, Michigan. In 1965, the dissolution of a bad partnership nearly wiped him out. Three years later fire destroyed $150,000 in company property, a significant portion of the business. Monaghan was insured, but the payoff equalled about ten cents on the dollar.

"Nothing is more common than unsuccessful men with talent."

-President Calvin Coolidge

Determined to succeed, Monaghan persevered. Even so, troubled financial times resulted in management of the business being assumed in 1970 by its chief creditor, a bank. When Monaghan was allowed to resume his position at the corporate helm he found more than 100 lawsuits waiting for him. To make matters worse, he owed $1.5 million to about 1,500 creditors.

Think that would give you a headache? Monaghan might think this would be putting it mildly. Nevertheless he kept working to make his business succeed.

His efforts paid off. He now has 3,300 branches of his chain business dispersed among every state in the United States. So the next time you receive an order delivered from a Domino's Pizza franchise, think of its founder, Thomas S. Monaghan, and his persistence. Without it you would have to call another pizza delivery service or, worse yet, go out and get one yourself!

A STEP AT A TIME

Once an elderly lady decided she would walk from New York City to Los Angeles, California, a distance of nearly 3,000 miles! Word of her plans attracted the attention of the news media and a reporter asked the woman how she thought she could ever make it from New York City to Los Angeles.

"One step at a time," the woman replied.

Like the great Chinese proverb says, every journey of a thousand miles begins with the first step. It is a proverb quoted so often that it is easy to ignore its fundamental wisdom. It is a proverb that best sums up any activity, whether it be cleaning our room or building a new company.

All great goals are achieved this way, and tackling your goals one step at a time is the best way to avoid getting discouraged. Don't look at the big picture except to set your goals and remind yourself periodically where you are going. The big picture motivates you and keeps you directed, but it is best to keep an eye on the place right in front of you in order to achieve the ultimate goals you have set.

Meaningful goals aren't achieved overnight; the goals must be broken down into individual steps, then each step must be executed.

A dieter faced with losing 50 pounds within a year might be overwhelmed by the task, while the thought of losing a pound per week may not frighten the dieter nearly as much; yet, both goals are the same if the latter goal is regularly reached. A would-be author might choke at the prospect of writing a 500-page book; but, if the author wrote only five pages per day the first draft would be completed in less than four months.

Keep working toward your goal; it may take a while to see results, but don't let that discourage you. After all, the captain of a ship travels at least 97 percent of a voyage without seeing the ship's goal or destination. Yet the captain nevertheless remains in charge of the ship; he or she doesn't get bored and quit.

Learn to stay the course.

DON'T BECOME OBSESSED

Keep your perspective when setting goals. You can't become a slave to them. A young Rockingham, North Carolina, girl, Kathryn Ormsby, was a junior distance runner at North Carolina State University when she came to Indianapolis, Indiana, to participate in a 10,000-meter race staged by the NCAA Track and Field Championships. Holding the collegiate record at the beginning of the race, she kept pace with the leaders when she suddenly ran off the track to a nearby bridge and jumped to the field below.

She survived, but she'll never walk – let alone run – again, according to her physicians, who diagnosed her as being permanently paralyzed by the fall. Her father offered the following explanation for this most uncharacteristic action by an outstanding athlete who also was valedictorian of her high school class: "I believe it had something to do with the pressure put on young people to succeed."

Setting big goals can lead to obsession. When a Japanese Air Lines plane crashed the president of the company resigned. If he had kept with age-old tradition he likely would have killed himself. Prior to World War II the common Japanese practice to atone for failure or disgrace was "harakiri," or ritualistic suicide by disembowelment. Although resignations have become the current norm, it is still not unheard of for Japanese citizens who perceive themselves as having failed to commit suicide.

Set reasonable yet challenging goals, the pursuit of which will give your life purpose, but won't tempt you to end your life if, at first, you don't succeed.

While visiting Hong Kong a few years ago, I toured a park that featured a high-rise structure, much higher than other buildings nearby. The top of the structure was accessible by stairway and offered sightseers a grand view of the city. I started the climb, but before I could reach the top, I saw it had been closed. I inquired why and was told by a park employee that it was exam time at local universities. The decision was made to close the observation deck to discourage suicidal students. I thought the employee was kidding me, but he explained that several students had recently flunked their final exams and had come to this structure to plunge to their deaths because they could not face failure.

The students evidently became obsessed with their goals and when they failed to achieve them they didn't want to live. This is a combination of obsession and a lack of a belief system. They obviously felt that they had failed and they lacked the belief to carry on. Self-belief is an essential ingredient to success; in fact, I'll devote the next three chapters to the need for building and maintaining a solid belief system.

The best way to guard against obsession is to make sure that you set goals for every area of your life. Set reasonable yet challenging goals, the pursuit of which will give your life purpose but won't tempt you to end your life if, at first, you don't succeed.

And, of course, you know what to do if that happens, right? Be persistent; try, try again.

After all, that's what dedication is all about.

CHAPTER SUMMARY

❖ To achieve or acquire something you don't have, you're going to have to sacrifice something you've already got. Significant goals require sacrifice.

❖ Obstacles are what you see when you take your eyes off your goal. The best way to avoid obstacles is to keep your eyes on your goal.

❖ It is wise to set big goals. Average goals may be relatively easy to obtain, but average is just as close to failing as succeeding.

❖ Persistence is essential to achieving your goals. While persistence won't necessarily assure you of achieving your goals, the absence of persistence will result in failure. Therefore, persistence is the best thing you'll have going for you.

❖ All significant goals are achieved one step at a time. Tackle your goals step by step. If you try to achieve them overnight, you'll likely become discouraged.

❖ Don't become obsessed with your goals, or frustration may result. Set goals in every area of your life to guard against obsession.

SECTION TWO
Belief

Belief: Unshakable confidence in your ability to achieve a goal. Ancient travelers moving across unknown or barren lands in search of food or shelter believed in their goal and trusted the markers left for them by other successful travelers. Travelers faced difficult passages and encountering an inukshuk gave the traveler unshakable confidence in following the direction of the marker. The fact that the landscape was still a threat and could cause them fear did not alter their confidence that if they followed the markers they would achieve their goal.

CHAPTER FIVE

You Can Succeed; Believe It!

Hollywood, 1933. A Metro-Goldwyn-Mayer testing director issued a memo in reference to the first screen test of a young dancer who was trying to make a name for himself. The memo read, "Can't act! Slightly bald! Can dance a little!"

Who was that testing director, anyhow? Fred Astaire knew. He kept that memo over the fireplace in his Beverly Hills home. The testing director didn't believe in Fred Astaire, but Astaire believed in himself and used the rejection to motivate and not discourage himself, and that's what made the difference.

Several years earlier, an unknown would-be actor by the name of James Cagney, who had yet to acquire motion picture fame, auditioned before noted musical playwright and Broadway star George M. Cohan for a part in one of his productions. Cohan wasn't impressed, and Cagney was dismissed on the spot.

In 1942, Cagney received his only Oscar for his starring performance in the blockbuster motion picture "Yankee Doodle Dandy" – the film biography of George M. Cohan. Cagney played the role only after Cohan (who apparently had forgotten Cagney's previous audition more than a decade earlier) gave his personal nod of approval.

> **Whenever you undertake anything new, your belief system is fragile by nature. You must offer yourself encouragement even when the world is ready to dismiss you as a failure.**

George M. Cohan didn't believe in James Cagney at first, but James Cagney did. As a result, Cohan later was to change his mind, much like theater critic Alexander Woolcott later did after publicly describing a young stage actor named Humphrey Bogart as simply "adequate." There's no shortage of such stories. A so-called expert once said of famed football coach Vince Lombardi: "He possesses minimal football knowledge. Lacks motivation." So much for experts!

Katherine Hepburn had a difficult time getting started as an actress. Some of her critics' complaints: "speaks too fast; nobody in the audience can understand her; too homely, too thin, too bony, too mannish; looks like a skeleton and has a voice like a rasp ... " She has since won four Academy Awards – a record that still stands today for any one performer! So much for the critics!

In 1832, a young man lost his job. Turning to politics, he was defeated in his bid for state legislature. Turning to self-employment, his business failed in 1833. Returning to politics, he was elected to the state legislature in 1834, but his political career got off to a less-than-impressive start; he suffered a nervous breakdown in 1836, having lost his sweetheart to death the year before.

After recovering, he lost elections for Speaker of the House in 1838 and for Congress in 1843. He was elected to Congress in 1846; his constituents, however, must not have been very impressed, because he lost a nomination bid for Congress two years later. He was rejected for land officer in 1849, defeated for the Senate in 1854, lost the vice presidency nomination in 1856 and was again defeated for the Senate in 1858.

Yet, despite all these so-called "failures," Abraham Lincoln was elected President of the United States in 1860, and has gone down in history as one of the greatest presidents of all time.

So respected did Lincoln become throughout the world that a statue of Lincoln was erected outside Westminster Abbey in London, among other places.

Even when no one else believed in him, Abraham Lincoln believed in Abraham Lincoln. As a result, the American voters changed their minds about him too.

Whenever you undertake anything new, your belief system is fragile by nature. You must offer yourself encouragement even when the world is ready to dismiss you as a failure.

Offering words of encouragement to would-be achievers in any and every field was the nation's 26th president, Theodore Roosevelt (who, interestingly, only became president when his predecessor, President William McKinley, was assassinated), he said: *"It's not the critic who counts; not the man who points out how the strongman stumbled, or where the doer of deeds could have done them better. The credit belongs to the man who is actually in the arena; who strives valiantly; who errs and comes up short again and again, because there is no effort without error and shortcoming: who does actually try to do the deed; who knows the great enthusiasm, the great devotion, knows in the end the triumph of high achievement, and who, at the worst, if he fails, at least fails while daring greatly. Far better is it to dare mighty things, to win glorious triumphs even though checkered by failure, than to rank with those poor spirits who neither enjoy nor suffer much because they live in the grey twilight that knows neither victory nor defeat."*

If you believe in yourself there's no limit to what you can do.

SUCCESS REQUIRES BELIEF

People who undertake anything challenging must believe in themselves if they are to succeed. Of course, believing in yourself won't guarantee your success, but not believing in yourself will indeed cause you to fail or, worse yet, quit.

The world is filled with critics and experts who are all too quick to point out your shortcomings. Unless you believe in yourself, you'll find yourself agreeing with them. If you do, you'll be your own worst enemy.

To me "failure" is just another challenge to succeed. It only becomes defeat when I make the conscious decision to quit. As long as I keep trying I haven't failed because I'm still trying.

People who believe in themselves generally will produce good results. They will at least offer their best efforts. This is true because people who believe in themselves feel good about themselves. They think they're worthy of succeeding and they usually keep trying until they do.

Take a lesson from the late Lee Liberace. An excellent entertainer who wowed audiences across America with his mastery of the keyboard and his flamboyant style, he offers these words on belief: *"One of the most important lessons I've learned is: Nobody will believe in you unless you believe in yourself first. If a person doubts his own ability, how can he convince others of his worth? I surround myself with positive-thinking people and try to remember that you always have to keep topping yourself."*

> To me, failure is just another challenge to succeed. It only becomes defeat when I make the conscious decision to quit. As long as I keep trying I haven't failed because I'm still trying.

On the other hand, people who chronically doubt their abilities to succeed do nothing but erode their own self-confidence and sabotage their own chances of success.

This will hurt them the next time they attempt the task, because they will dwell on their previous failure rather than concentrating on succeeding. Rather than try to top themselves, their negative thought-process will cause them to live down to all their negative expectations.

This is a shame, because failure really isn't such a bad thing. In fact, it's an essential ingredient of success.

IT MIGHT NOT FEEL GOOD, BUT IT'S A START

No one likes to fail. Some even think it is un-American to fail. Our society places so much emphasis on winning that failure seems almost synonymous with disgrace or disease. Consequently, many people feel it's better not to try at all than to try and fail.

It is rare, indeed, when anyone can attempt anything for the first time and succeed. When a novice masters a feat right away, it is generally because he or she possesses a great deal of knowledge, skill and experience in a related area.

While failure is nothing to celebrate, it isn't evil. Failure is an essential ingredient of success, because we learn by failing. Let me give you a personal example.

I knew absolutely zero about skiing prior to a few years ago except that it looked exciting. I had met John Goddard (the adventuresome goal setter I mentioned in a previous chapter) and he inspired me to set bigger and more exciting goals. To someone who has never skied before the prospect of skiing down a mountainside seemed a fairly exciting goal to set.

So off I went with my family and a couple of friends to Denver, Colorado. At sunrise after the night we arrived, I was ready to tackle the mountain, much like a college boy is ready to tackle the world on his first day on the job – before he's had a chance to discover that the world doesn't tackle easily.

IT WAS ALL DOWNHILL FROM THERE

I rushed to put on my ski boots. There was my first sign of trouble; the boots were too small. One of the employees kindly informed me that he thought my boots would fit perfectly – if I would remove my street boots first!

I laughed, but not nearly as heartily as several other employees, who stood nearby with fingers pointed in my direction, amused by my ignorance.

After my boots were fastened I went outside to tackle the mountain. My young daughter, Alicia, also was eager to get started.

"I already know how to ski because I've been twice before," Alicia said.

I watched Alicia skiing down the small hill upon which beginners are taught. It looked so easy. I put on my skis, however, and found that I couldn't move.

"They don't go uphill, Bill," said my instructor, a very charming and confident woman named Sue. "You've got to learn to walk in them. Like this, see?"

THEN IT WAS ALL UPHILL

She started walking sideways uphill, thrusting the edge of her left ski into the snow, then bringing the edge of her right ski just below it. Then she lifted her left leg uphill and thrust the edge of that ski into the snow, bringing her right leg up to her left leg, just like before.

"This is how you walk up a hill," Sue said. "You try it, Bill." Looked easy to me. I gave it a try. Then I got up off the snow-covered ground.

"Great!" she said. "You're doing fine." "Sure," I said, taking another step, only to wind up back in the snow. "Hey, you even fall good!" "Thanks a lot," I said.

"No, I mean it," she said. "You fall very nicely. I have a feeling that's going to be a plus for you."

I was beginning to have second thoughts. Perhaps my

place was in the ski lodge sitting before a roaring fire and sipping on a cup of hot cider. Then I thought of the money I had invested in this trip – $500 times four to outfit myself, my wife Joanna, and my two daughters. Add to that the $250 per night it was costing us to stay at a nearby condominium and I decided against an afternoon at the fireplace, it was out of my price range.

I persevered. Finally, I made it to the top of the ten-foot learner's slope. I pushed off with my poles and started skiing down the track, running off it long before it ran out. I tasted more snow.

This went on for two hours. My only thoughts were, "I'm tired of falling and walking sideways up the hill so I can fall again. I want to ski!" I had forgotten that failure was essential to success.

Giving me an emotional boost was Sue. She repeatedly encouraged me as I progressed from the learner's slope and on to the ski-lift. One can't help but get a little squeamish while waiting for a cold metal bench zipping by to snatch you off the ground and into the air much like an outfielder would scoop up a baseball.

I continued to progress the rest of the day and I had the bruises to prove it. And when the next sunrise presented itself "sore" didn't begin to describe the way I felt. In fact, if we hadn't rented the skis for two days I might have decided that I could have afforded the fireplace's heat after all; it might have been cheaper than an emergency helicopter flight to a Denver hospital, which is where it felt at times I might be heading.

Once on the slopes, however, a hospital was the farthest thing from my mind. While I'm sure that my form and style left something to be desired, I nevertheless found myself skiing down the slopes without falling, without stopping ... For an Indiana flatland man, that's success!

Then I heard, "Hey, Bill, you are doing super!"

I turned to see who was talking to me. It was Sue, my instructor from the previous day. She was still encouraging me. Then she did something that caused my confidence to soar. She asked me to escort a novice on the lift up the slope.

In effect, I became the instructor, helping the beginner with the problems I had experienced the day before, such as how to get on and off the lift and how to fall without stabbing yourself with a ski pole.

THE FOUR STAGES OF BELIEF

For anything you would attempt, there are four stages of belief through which you evolve. Let's review them.

Unconscious incompetent.

The person has yet to try the task, but holds high expectations for his or her ability to master it. Though devoid of experience he or she is eager and enthusiastic.

I was experiencing this stage on the first morning of our ski trip. I arose at 6 a.m. and woke my family and friends. I was ready to ski! This stage started to fade when I attempted to cram my street boots into my ski boots, and it disappeared completely when I tried to walk uphill sideways.

Conscious incompetent.

This is the next stage, and I entered this one after I realized that I had a lot to learn about skiing. Many people quit at this point; it was at this point that I considered retreating to the lodge. People who do stay with the task upon reaching this stage fully understand that mastering it will be a challenge. This stage stuck with me for pretty much the rest of my first day on the slopes.

Conscious competent.

I didn't reach this stage on the trip, but I was nevertheless satisfied with my progress. The ability to ski down a one and one-half mile slope was a triumph in itself for me. It took every bit of my concentration to accomplish this feat. When I can do it without falling or stopping, I will reach the stage of conscious competent.

Unconscious competent.

I probably won't live long enough to reach this stage on the ski slopes, although when it comes to collecting debts I've been at this stage for some time. If I had reached this stage as a skier, I would have been able to zip expertly down the slope while thinking about what I had for dinner the night before. Once a person reaches this stage he has reached the goal and is ready for more demanding challenges.

Failing is only failure when you quit.

Nobody likes failing. Remember, though, that failing is only failure when you quit. I could have failed as a skier by retreating to the fireplace but I didn't. Instead I persevered and turned my failings into successes.

The person who would try anything new must be willing to risk embarrassment because he or she must go through the conscious incompetent stage to succeed. There's no way around it.

By the same token, it's important to experience and recognize these four stages of belief whenever you undertake anything new. In so doing you won't take failing personally and you will be able to maintain your enthusiasm for mastering the task.

Of course, the person who would enjoy true success must realize that the conscious competency stage is only a sign of progress. Consistently smooth execution of any task depends on the person becoming an unconscious competent. People reach that stage only after "paying their dues," so to speak.

The only way you can pay your dues is by believing and doing. The next chapter will offer more discussion on this.

CHAPTER SUMMARY

❖ People who undertake anything challenging must believe in themselves if they are to succeed. People who chronically doubt their abilities to succeed do nothing but erode their own self-confidence and sabotage their own chances of success.

❖ Failure is an essential ingredient of success, because we learn by failing.

❖ There are four stages of belief we must experience when we try anything new. They are unconscious incompetent, conscious incompetent, conscious competent and unconscious competent. The second stage is the most frightening. People who reach this stage make the active decision either to quit or to persevere.

CHAPTER SIX

Dare To Believe

Children have great belief systems. A child who takes "no" for an answer probably is just thinking of a way to rephrase their question because they believe they can get what they want if they try hard enough.

If you don't believe me just take a child to the grocery store with you and walk down the aisle that displays cereals. With the possible exception of cookies (also a favorite with children), cereals take up more shelf space than any other item in the store.

And if you can walk past the cereal aisle without picking up a box for the child, you're a better person than I am.

Every time I took my children to the grocery store I knew I was in for trouble when we reached the cereals. I would favor something healthy and nutritious, such as Raisin Bran or Shredded Wheat. My children would favor a brand that bordered on junk food, generally made of chocolate and often sprinkled with marshmallows.

It didn't take me long to figure out that it was better for them to have the brand they preferred rather than spend great deals of time and energy proving my point – to deaf ears, I might add – and paying for it by not getting any good-night kisses from them for a week.

Yes, children are great believers. With curious minds they tackle the impossible and aren't too discouraged by failures.

Sometime in their adolescence their belief system starts to weaken because they start a bad habit that, many times, they never stop.

The habit? Worrying. Suddenly, their confidence begins to fade, eroded by worry that is mostly devoted to their perceived inadequacies. Their outlook tends to suffer. When they become old enough to lose their childlike innocence, they tend to devote too much attention to the negative aspects of life, which fuels their worry about the prospect of a grim future.

According to a USA Today poll of 8,000 pre-teen children aged 10 to 11, these pre-teens have a variety of things to worry about. They worry mostly about grades: at least, 56 percent of the respondents said they did. Other topics included looks, 53 percent; popularity, 48 percent; USA hunger and poverty, 38 percent; USA violence. 36 percent; drugs and alcohol abuse, 35 percent ; and nuclear destruction of the USA, 25 percent.

Isn't this astounding? If the poll is accurate, one out of four of these pre-teens in the U.S. between the ages of 10 and 11 has serious doubts about the future of our country.

A young child isn't preoccupied with himself or herself, or with what's happening across the globe, or even across town, for that matter. A young child doesn't have image problems, doubts about self-worth and anxieties over the fate of the world.

This isn't to say that some children don't have problems. But generally, a child just believes ... and believes and believes ... It's only when he or she approaches adolescence that he or she learns to doubt and fear ... and those two villains can destroy belief.

Of course, we can't remain children forever. But if we could just carry the belief systems that we have as children over into our adult lives we would be so much more productive and happier.

Unfortunately, that isn't realistic in many cases. So the second best thing is to redevelop our belief systems.

HOW TO BUILD BELIEF

Why do children have such strong belief systems? One reason is simply because adults offer strong encouragement. When a baby takes a first step all types of praise usually are forthcoming from the adults in the child's life. The same holds true when a baby drinks out of a cup for the first time, or when a small child learns to dress and tie his or her shoes.

It's amazing how we as adults bestow praise on a small child. Yet we all too often refuse to give praise to older people when it is needed just as badly. For example, an adult who is working his or her first day on a new job (especially one in a new field) may not have a strong belief system and could badly use the seeds of praise to get it started. As it has been said, "praise what you want to raise." If a person (child or adult) is praised for behaving and or performing properly, he or she will have the encouragement to continue to do so.

Adults also find it difficult to generate self-belief because they tend to be too tough on themselves. They sometimes expect to start a new job with little if any difficulty, which often is simply unrealistic. Like a baby learning to walk, it will take time to "learn the ropes," so to speak. A belief system can be built if someone in authority is willing to praise worthwhile efforts and good performances. I doubt very much that I would have learned to ski had Sue, my ski instructor, withheld her praise or, worse, been critical of my initial attempts.

Many times, however, a person won't have someone to praise him or her when needed. Therefore, the person will have to build a belief system without help. Here is some advice on building a belief system you can use should you ever find yourself in that position.

Commit yourself to a life-long learning process.

As an old saying goes, "When you think you're no longer green, you're not ripe; you're rotten!" Keep learning; it can't hurt and virtually always will help.

As Helen Keller noted, *"Knowledge is power. Rather, knowledge is happiness, because to have knowledge – broad, deep knowledge – is to know true ends from false, and lofty things from low. To know the thoughts and deeds that have marked man's progress is to feel the great heartthrobs of humanity through the centuries; and if one does not feel in these pulsations a heavenward striving, one must indeed be deaf to the harmonies of life."*

Participate in the decisions we make for our future.

A plan doesn't become reality until it is acted upon. To

put it simply, don't waste too much time thinking about taking on the task and take it on! You can't succeed until you try.

Recognize yourself when you succeed or progress.

It's important that you are praised for your progress. And it's nice to have someone else recognize you for good performances. But for various reasons this isn't always realistic. So a little encouragement even if it's only from yourself can go a long way to building belief.

Provide opportunity for growth.

To strengthen a belief system it's important to keep getting better. As I pointed out in the previous chapter, an unconscious competent will get bored with a job and possibly start making careless mistakes unless he or she is presented with new challenges. People need challenges to keep growing; the alternative is stagnation. Every time you succeed, your belief system is strengthened.

Let these four pointers be your guide for building a solid belief system. It's essential that you have one to be successful.

SELF-DOUBT IS WASTE

Some people are so busy doubting themselves that they don't have time to believe. If they would spend some of that time believing and trying instead of doubting they'd at least be doing something constructive. At most they'd be working their way toward success.

A person who doubts his or her own abilities isn't likely to stop doubting until he or she at least tests them. Then the person can stop doubting. Either the person will know that he or she truly can succeed at the task in question or he or she will know that, at least for now, he or she can't succeed and is in need of more practice and/or training.

Self-doubt simply is a waste of time. A group of eleven mountain climbers led by Phil Bartow didn't waste their time doubting whether they could reach the 14,410-foot peak of Mt. Ranier, Washington, in July 1981 one month after an icefall buried alive 11 climbers there. They just went ahead and started the climb.

Nine of the eleven climbers made it a day ahead of schedule, two dropped out because of illnesses.

The fact that the two dropouts were blind had nothing to do with the fact that they didn't reach the peak. Of the nine who succeeded, six were blind, two were deaf and one had only one leg; he climbed with an artificial limb.

The handicapped mountain climbers could have spent their time doubting. Who could have blamed them? However, they decided to spend their time trying – and succeeding.

Alan Landin of Texas doesn't have time to doubt, either. He was blinded by an industrial accident at an oil rig when a malfunctioning machine backed by 2,000 pounds of pressure pumped automatic transmission fluid through his eye socket. Doctors thought his brain had been too badly contaminated for Alan ever to function again, if he even was to survive at all.

He was home within three weeks after the accident, however, because he believed – first in God, second in himself. He had a wife and two children at home that he loved spending time with. He had too much to lose by doubting. He says the reason he was able to survive is because his life was sustained by his strong religious faith and the encouragement he received from fellow members of the Texas A & M Church of Christ.

He keeps busy, among other things, by reading. Although he can no longer see, he listens to cassette tapes of motivational speakers and novels. Charged by the inspirational speakers who Alan said has made a difference in his life, he learned how to read braille and now helps others cope who have been similarly injured.

Alan doesn't have time to doubt; he's simply too busy.

Scott Hagara of Indianapolis believes in himself. His personal record for the Revco Marathon in Indianapolis was 2 hours and 49 minutes (pretty good given that the world record is only a little less at 2 hours, 4 minutes and 26 seconds – set by 34-year-old Ethiopian Haile Gebrelassie Sept. 30, 2007, at the Berlin Marathon). Hagara entered the annual event the year following his personal best and finished in two hours, 50 minutes and 54 seconds, his second-best time ever. He didn't break his record, but it's interesting to note that his second-best time was set with Hagara in a wheelchair. He had lost the use of his legs in an automobile accident the previous year and his arms did the "running" in this marathon instead of his legs.

Hagara didn't have time to doubt; he knew that success takes many forms. Rather than lament his inability to compete on foot he strove for success in a wheelchair, training for the event by lifting weights.

Kathy Miller of Scottsdale, Arizona, was almost killed in 1977 when the 16-year-old was struck by an automobile with such impact that it literally knocked her out of her shoes. Doctors held little hope for her survival and virtually no hope for her being anything more than a vegetable if she did survive. Eight months later Kathy entered and completed a six mile foot race as her friends and supporters cheered her on.

She couldn't afford to doubt; she was too busy putting her life back together.

New York model Marla Hanson's pretty face was slashed with a razor by two thugs hired by a revenge-seeking landlord angered over an $850 security deposit dispute. The prospect of living life with a deformed face might have caused many models to withdraw from the world; some even might have committed suicide because of their inability to adapt. Marla Hanson went on living, vowing that if plastic surgeons couldn't restore her face, she would pursue another profession.

John Goddard, the multiple goal setter and achiever I discussed earlier in this book, was stricken with abdominal cancer in 1983. A very painful and often fatal affliction, Goddard nevertheless beat "the big C." He credits his survival to his strong will to live and determination that "I wasn't going to let this overcome me."

That indeed took courage, because there were others present who weren't very good role models. After four "extremely painful" surgeries, Goddard said he was walking about the hospital ward and passed three rooms occupied by men who suffered from the same affliction. They were dying.

"I investigated and found that to them, in their own minds, cancer was synonymous with death. You know, they thought, 'You've got cancer, you're going to die!' So these jerks were lying there full of self-pity, dying by degree and I couldn't even get their doctors to motivate them to get out of the sack and get on with their lives. They just had lost the will to live and are probably dead now."

Goddard refused to be negative, despite the seriousness

of his situation. Through positive thinking and faith he refused to give up. It paid off. His cancer went into remission and he continues checking off items on his list of life's goals.

"I sincerely believe in faith, "Goddard said. "I feel like Jesus heals through that faith. Faith unlocks tremendous strength. Once you get that confidence and that hope of survival, half the battle is won right there."

John Goddard could have chosen to doubt, but he chose to live instead.

> **Why do some people fail at such small tasks when other people can overcome obstacles that could cause giants to stumble? The answer is as simple as it is sad: They don't believe in themselves.**

All of these people chose to believe because they found the alternatives unacceptable. Yet, I've had the experience of seeing people fail at tasks that pale in comparison. I watched a 43-year-old woman with a master's degree fail at her job because she doubted her ability to learn how to operate a computer! I also saw a large, six-foot-two man reduced to human jelly over a similar situation. He went back to college to learn about computers when all he needed was to learn the basics of computer operation – a job that required minimal skills. The man ultimately quit his job because of lack of confidence.

Why did these people fail at such small tasks when other people can overcome obstacles that could cause giants to stumble? The answer is as simple as it is sad: They didn't believe in themselves.

When a person engages in self-doubt, his or her belief system is going to take a beating. With that in mind, self-doubt is more than just a waste; it's destructive as well!

When we find ourselves filled with self-doubt we should think of John Goddard, Kathy Miller, Scott Hagara, Alan Landin, the handicapped mountain climbers and many others like them who have developed and benefited from such strong belief systems. Perhaps we could benefit by their examples.

BY THE INCH, NOT THE YARD

Many people recoil at the prospect of doing something new, and not just when the task may seem insurmountably difficult. Change is frightening. In short, the conscious incompetent stage hits them like a ton of bricks and crushes their belief system.

If you should face a similar problem, perhaps it would help you to remember how you build a belief system in a child. Take sledding for example, a child might be hesitant to ride a sled for the first time because the experience is totally new to him or her. As a result, he or she may be afraid of falling, or simply frightened of the ride itself.

Yet, most children enjoy sledding because an adult helps them build their belief systems. First, the adult might pull the child on the sled. Next, the adult may set the child up for a ride down a small hill. Then the adult may accompany the child for a ride down a larger hill.

At this point, the child will likely go it alone because he or she has been shown that a sled ride won't hurt. As a result the child may take and even enjoy all sorts of falls and tumbles for the rest of the day because he or she has been shown that sledding can be a lot of fun.

Yet consider the child's likely reaction had he or she been introduced to sledding by a solo run down a steep hill. The experience likely would have been too much for the child to digest all at once. As a result he or she might have been very hesitant to get on the sled again.

This same lesson applies to adults. If they are plunged head-first into a new experience, they may be overcome by fear. On the other hand, if they take on the task one step at a time they'll likely succeed because they will be willing to persevere, encouraged by a series of small successes.

To sum it up in a sentence, I'll borrow a line from Dr. Robert Schuller: "Yard by yard, life is hard. Inch by inch, it's a cinch."

Take anything new one step at a time to minimize fear and maximize self-confidence.

CONCEIVE AND BELIEVE

Just remember what William James, often called the father of psychology, said in the early 20th century: "Whatever the mind can conceive and believe, it can achieve."

Your mind is powerful; when coupled with determination guided by belief there is no limit to what you can do.

Successful people build belief systems that get them started toward their goals. They know that believing is critical to the success formula.

If you find it difficult to develop belief, perhaps there is something that you fear that is standing in your way. If this is the case, don't be ashamed. We're all afraid of something. But don't let let the fear stand in your way. Step around it, over it, dig under it, build a plane and fly over it! Or get a friend who understands and have them walk with you through it. Just don't let it put an end to you before you try.

Don't live in fear. Successful people are successful because they do what they fear. If fear is a real part of your life, you'll find the next chapter interesting. In it, I'll offer some advice that will help you get the best of your fear, before it gets the best of you.

CHAPTER SUMMARY

❖ Children have strong belief systems that tend to weaken as they age. As adults, we often find it necessary to redevelop our belief systems, for we need strong ones to succeed.

❖ The steps of building a successful belief system include committing yourself to a life-long learning process, participating in the decisions we make for your future, recognizing yourself when you succeed and providing opportunity for personal and/or professional growth.

❖ Self-doubt is a waste of time because it results in inaction.

❖ When a person engages in self-doubt, his or her belief system is going to take a beating. With that in mind, self-doubt is more than just a waste; it's destructive as well!

❖ When building your belief system, don't take too much too soon. Take anything new one step at a time to minimize fear and maximize self-confidence.

❖ As noted psychiatrist William James noted in the early part of the 20th century, "Whatever the mind can conceive and believe, it can achieve."

CHAPTER SEVEN

Conquer Fears And Other Foes

People tend to have all types of reasons for not believing in themselves. I'm not sure that any of them are good reasons.

Some people don't believe in themselves because they may believe they are too old, too young, too poor, or too dependent on a particular lifestyle to risk it for success. Some people believe they don't have enough talent or intelligence, while others believe they simply wouldn't stand a chance because they believe that bad luck follows them like their shadows.

I could go on and on with all types of reasons why people don't believe in themselves, but I'm sure you get the picture. The interesting thing about all of this is that many of these same people are willing to believe in lots of other things

– almost anything, in fact – except themselves.

It just goes to show that people are going to believe in something. Instead of believing in their abilities to succeed, most people choose to believe in self-imposed barriers that block their paths to success. And people who believe they can't succeed usually don't succeed. They convince themselves they can't, so they don't even try.

Sometimes these barriers are based on fact; a person with a serious heart condition probably shouldn't undertake a marathon run. That's prudence. On the other hand, they may be mere excuses to cover for the fact that the person is simply afraid to try. And fear should never stop a person from trying.

FEAR – THE NUMBER ONE FOE TO BELIEF

The lack of belief or the fear of failure can figuratively crush even the strongest of people. Fear is clearly the enemy of belief. Fear itself may be considered an acronym standing for "False Emotions Appearing Real." Fear is what people experience when they dwell on the worst-case scenario, regardless of how likely that is to occur.

For example, it isn't realistic to be afraid of air travel and not afraid of other modes of travel when you look at fatality statistics. For every 10 billion highway passenger miles traveled there are 94 deaths related to automobile accidents. For every 10 billion rail miles traveled, 4 deaths. For every 10 billion air passenger miles traveled there is only one death related to airline crashes. In short, the odds of being killed in a car crash are about 95 times higher than they are for dying in an airline accident. It is maybe only because airline crashes attract wide-spread media attention that some people are afraid to fly.

Fear has been called the darkroom where negative thoughts are developed. In the case of the person who is afraid of flying, his or her lack of information amounts to a "darkroom." The negative thought of increased odds for death is the result of a lack of information.

With that in mind, the "light" of knowledge can eliminate the "darkroom" and the "negative thoughts" as well. It has often been said that knowledge is the antidote to fear.

If you are afraid of something, learn about it. The more you know about the subject the less you'll fear it

COPE WITH FEAR

Fear is a strong force; but it is also one that must be dealt with if the fear interferes with your success goals. For example, a person won't need to be rid of a fear of snakes if his career and personal life doesn't involve them. On the other hand, an executive who must travel frequently by air to perform his or her job had best learn to handle a fear of flying. If not, he will be out of work pretty quickly.

Fear may be considered an acronym standing for False Emotions Appearing Real.

Fear is not something that will go away on its own any more than courage comes automatically. Courage is not the absence of fear; at least it isn't the way I define it. Instead, courage is the ability to act positively and productively even though the environment or situation might cause you to be afraid. Sometimes fear is the very thing that is needed to prompt courage. But a person still has to get past the fear.

This might be a good place to tell you how I once fought off a whole platoon of enemy soldiers armed with only a pistol. But the fact is, my obligation to Uncle Sam never took me to a battlefield. So I'll have to settle for something less colorful, perhaps a story of being in a metropolitan city in with my daughter, Alicia, when she was younger. It's not a heroic war tale, but it will do for illustrating this section.

Alicia and I were walking down a street that didn't seem as friendly as I might have liked (in this particular city, this could have been any street). Yet, we had to get where we were going and driving a car wasn't practical. Therefore, we walked, passing various unsavory-looking characters along the way. A little nervous, maybe, Alicia asked me if I ever was afraid of anything, to which I told her that as long as I kept my eyes open and was fairly aware of what was going on around me, I have a good chance of taking care of myself. Thankfully I didn't have to have my words tested that day. We arrived where we were going without incident.

That's the way to deal with fear. Be prepared for the challenge that could cause you fear. If a challenge exposes you to a fearful situation you have two options: Either retreat or be aware and be prepared to act as conditions warrant. It is always better to be prepared.

Let's boil this down to a step-by-step process.

Measure the difficulty of the challenge.

If the prospect of performing a particular task or assignment causes you fear, assess the difficulty involved. You've faced challenges in the past; compare those with the new one to determine just how difficult by comparison the new task is.

Bring past successes into the present.

Of your past challenges, how many of those ended in success? Count them. The more successes you've realized the greater confidence you'll develop. As it has been said, competence creates confidence.

Imagine the worst-case scenario that could result.

Is it commensurate with the challenge? Could you live with it should it come to pass? For example, if the challenge involved the investing of large sums of your money, could you live with a 100 percent loss? It's important for you to be aware of what could happen even if the odds may be as small as dying in an airline crash.

Be prepared.

Before you undertake any challenge it's best to be prepared. Although we've already established that failure isn't necessarily bad, it is still to be avoided if possible. One way to avoid failure is to be prepared for the challenge. As it has often been said, luck is preparation meeting opportunity. Also, preparation can make up for a lack of natural talent. If the challenge requires skill that doesn't come naturally preparation can minimize if not eliminate your disadvantage.

Visualize yourself succeeding.

This is important. Your ability to produce positive results will be enhanced by a visual image of success. By the same token your chances of failing will be increased by a mental picture of failure. Convince yourself first that you can succeed, then show the rest of the world that you can.

Act confidently.

The best way to convince yourself – and the rest of the world as well – that you can succeed is to act confidently. Remind yourself at every opportunity that you can succeed, especially when success seems to be out of reach.

Make an unapologetic commitment.

Commit yourself to success by telling others about your commitment to succeed. Speak positively about your belief that you can succeed. This isn't false confidence or arrogance. Your commitment might draw encouragement from your friends. On the other hand, it might prompt smirks and giggles from some, jeers and taunts from others. However, such responses will make you more determined than ever to succeed if for no other reason but to prove your critics wrong.

Courage is the ability to act positively and productively even though the environment or situation might cause you to be afraid.

Recognize your good performances.

Complimenting people for their good performances is a sound strategy for building confidence in others. The same strategy will work for you. When you've done a good job and you know it, celebrate it. Give yourself a pat on the back and a reward as well.

Follow this plan to the letter when facing a challenge that causes you fear. To be afraid is no shame; all of us are afraid of something. However, to let fear control you is a waste of your potential – a waste that you very possibly may live to regret.

OTHER BARRIERS TO BELIEF

Fear isn't the only thing that stands in our way to success. Sometimes we place other limitations upon ourselves, which I mentioned earlier in this chapter. As I said then, these reasons may be excuses to cover for the fact that we're afraid. On the other hand these barriers to belief may be real because we perceive them to be real. Let's take a deeper look at them.

Lack of knowledge and/or experience.

This might be the biggest reason many people don't undertake more challenges; they feel that they're not sufficiently skilled or knowledgeable to meet the challenge. Of course you wouldn't attempt brain surgery if you have absolutely no background in medicine, but it's highly unrealistic you would even desire to undertake such a challenge under such circumstances. Most challenges you might desire to undertake probably are within your grasp if you're willing to do what it takes to succeed. A lack of knowledge is no excuse, simply because of the rich heritage we've inherited from our forefathers. Libraries are full of the knowledge you might need to succeed; the same can be said of older, more experienced people that we might know. You can face a challenge confidently – even though you may not know all that you need to know to meet it – because the knowledge you'll need is readily available.

Past failures.

When it comes to meeting the challenge of love, many

people run away from it. Because they've failed at love in the past, they aren't willing to experience again the pain that failure might bring. Of course, they are the big losers because they cheat themselves out of the joy that love can bring. The same is true with any type of challenge. If your past failures have persuaded you to avoid future challenges you are cheating yourself out of the rewards that success could bring. Remember, failure isn't really failure until you stop trying to succeed; as long as you're trying, failure is merely a lesson. Learn from your failures, and you'll increase your chances of success.

Lack of money.

This has been a barrier to many people's belief systems, but it shouldn't be. If you have a marketable plan or idea that has the potential for profit, you should be able to find a financial backer who can help you on your path to success. Don't try to be a self-made person, because there is no such animal. No one is going to succeed unless a lot of other people want him or her to succeed.

Age.

You're never too old to succeed; success isn't reserved for people under the age of forty. Col. Harland Sanders wasn't too old to parlay his Kentucky Fried Chicken recipe into a multi-million dollar business, although he was 65 plus when he started. Winston

> You are never too old to succeed; success isn't reserved for people under the age of forty.

Churchill had experienced a life filled with problems and setbacks until he became England's prime minister at the age of 62. Twenty years later he undertook and completed his four volume work, A History Of The English Speaking Peoples. Arthur Rubenstein gave one of his greatest recitals in New York's Carnegie Hall – at the age of 89. At the age of 92, Adolph Zukor was still chairman of the board at Paramount Pictures. You're never too old to succeed.

Opinions of others.

Many people have been discouraged from succeeding by taking to heart the opinions of others, many of whom were unqualified to give advice in the first place. Even those who are qualified to criticize can be wrong. Actor Jack Nicholson's manager told him in the early 1960s to find another line of work; if Nicholson had taken his advice, someone else would have won the Oscar for Best Actor of 1976. It's often good to talk with others about our plans for success, but not if we're going to let them talk us out of trying.

If you have another barrier to belief that I haven't mentioned, I would suggest that you take a deeper look at it. Once you recognize it for what it is, you'll be able to break through it, clearing the way for your first step toward success.

THE IMPOSSIBLE JOB WAS POSSIBLE

Do you think you could prepare and serve dinner for 100,000? The late Daddy Bruce Randolph thought he could, and he didn't mind giving it a try.

Daddy Bruce owned and operated Daddy Bruce's Barbecue in Denver. Daddy Bruce became so popular for his efforts to take on the improbable that the municipal powers changed the name of Denver's 34th Avenue to Bruce Randolph Boulevard. While he was still living!

He made the front page of USA Today in late 1985 because he took on the task of feeding 100,000 people on Thanksgiving Day. What's more, he succeeded! Some customers paid, others who were needy ate on the house. In all, 100,000 plates of barbecue were dished out that day.

This was a job that could have challenged, if not outright frightened, the strongest of people. Daddy Bruce did it. He met the physical, mental and emotional demands of arranging dinner for 100,000.

He was 81 years old at the time.

On a trip to Denver, I decided that I had to meet this man. On November 6, 1986 – almost a year after he staged the big feed to end all big feeds – I had dinner at Daddy Bruce's Barbecue. It was a popular restaurant for two reasons. One, the food was simply delicious, and two, a waitress named Peaches told me that "everybody loves Daddy Bruce."

After I met him, I found out why everyone loves him. He helps people. He said he loves helping people even more than he loves the Denver Broncos football team. He has been so active with civic and community affairs that the mayor of Denver sent him a letter proclaiming him a good neighbor since 1963, the year he opened his restaurant at the age of 59 – a time when most people are planning to retire.

Daddy Bruce was a black man from Arkansas who believed he could make a difference in people's lives and he didn't let age or skin color stand in his way. His beliefs wouldn't let him. When most of the nation was caught up in the civil rights discussion, Daddy Bruce was living proof a man's rights simply by living by those rights. Daddy Bruce believed in the right to succeed and to also treat others the way he wanted to be treated.

If you're in Denver and want to see his belief in action, go visit his restaurant. His family is still all there.

MEET YOUR CHALLENGES

If Daddy Bruce could pack up and move to a new city and start a new business when he was nearly 60 years old, what challenge faces you that you can't at least try to meet?

It has been said that problems are nothing more than opportunities in disguise. It's mostly a matter of attitude. The next chapter, the first under the section of control, deals specifically with controlling your attitude. When you can do this, you'll be amazed at the opportunities that abound in your life.

CHAPTER SUMMARY

❖ The lack of belief, or the fear of failure, can figuratively crush even the strongest of people.

❖ Cope with fear. Measure the difficulty of the challenge. Bring past successes into the present. Imagine the worst-case scenario that could result. Be prepared. Visualize yourself succeeding. Act confidently. Make an unapologetic commitment. Recognize your good performances.

❖ Other barriers to belief include self-imposed limitations, such as lack of knowledge and/or experience, past failures, lack of money, age and opinions of others.

SECTION THREE
Control

Control: The ability to direct your attitude, actions, and appearance.

The path was not always well marked. Weather and time took their toll on some markers. Sometimes the ancient traveler found they were the first traveler and had to build an inukshuk where none before existed. When the way was unclear the ancient traveler might be tempted to lose control, complain, or even quit. They might be tempted by despair to ignore important repairs to their clothes or hunting gear. Such losses of control could be fatal so most travelers maintained their control by guarding their attitudes, action, and appearance. When the hunter returned successfully to their village they were well-clothed and carrying caches of life-sustaining goods. More often than not they also left behind them new inuksuit for future hunters and travelers.

CHAPTER EIGHT

Taming Your Attitude

Many people consider Robert Louis Stevenson's classic work *The Strange Case Of Dr. Jekyll And Mr. Hyde* to be only science fiction. While there is no concoction I know of that instantly alters a person's physical appearance, I've watched many people change from well-respected citizens to obnoxious boors in a matter of moments by downing a few glasses of alcohol.

This chapter is not a sermon on the evils of booze. It is, however., about how a person can allow outside influences to affect their attitude. And the power of a person's attitude and how it can make the difference between success and failure is illustrated in this famous story.

Dr. Henry Jekyll knew that human beings have two tendencies within themselves – positive and negative. By the time the good doctor discovered that the tendency that we feed is the one that leads, it was too late for him to save himself. His negative soul – Edward Hyde – already had taken control of his life. As a result, Henry Jekyll lost everything – his practice, his respectability and ultimately his very life.

It wasn't the strange potion that did him in; instead, Henry Jekyll was a victim of his own attitude.

ATTITUDE – THE LAST FREEDOM

Imagine that an enemy conquered America and occuppied our country with military forces. Not a nice thought, I'll agree, but let's imagine that our country ceased to be a free nation. We could lose our freedom of speech, our freedom to work and worship as we choose, and our freedom to pursue happiness in the fashion that we please. Despite the loss of those freedoms there would still be one freedom that couldn't be taken away from us. When we lose this freedom it's only because we willingly cast it aside.

> "The last of the human freedoms is to choose one's attitude in any given set of circumstances."
> --Victor Frankl

This freedom is the ability to choose our attitudes. As noted psychologist Victor Frankl said, "The last of the human freedoms is to choose one's attitude in any given set of circumstances." Frankl was a Jew who had been imprisoned in a concentration camp in Germany during World War II.

He survived while others died, and he attributes his survival to his having learned to have a different attitude about things he had no control over.

We can't control everything that happens to us but we most certainly can control our reaction to events that affect us. In so doing we determine our destiny. We can react either positively or negatively to a misfortune. Of course the person who chooses to react positively will benefit from the experience in some way, be it large or small, while the person who reacts negatively likely won't benefit at all.

ANYONE CAN HAVE A GOOD ATTITUDE

When we choose our attitudes, we are practicing the most basic freedom that all human beings enjoy, regardless of where they live and what government influences them.

> The tendency you feed is the tendency that leads.

Anyone can have a good attitude regardless of their situation. In fact, many times a person's lot in life is actually determined by his or her attitude. In a previous chapter in the section on dedication I mentioned that some people choose not to be dedicated because they are dissatisfied with their career situations. These people choose to have negative attitudes and they're often penalized for it. They make the conscious decision not to do the things it will take to make them successful and they must pay the price for it. It matters not how unfairly they may have been treated by their employers or co-workers; they made the decision to react negatively to a situation and they must stand to reap what results from their decision.

Consider the difference had they made the decision to react differently. Even though they may have felt they were treated unfairly, suppose they reacted positively by working diligently. They would have at least increased their chances of reaping rewards from good performances because they developed better skills that either would lead to a promotion or to a better job altogether.

I can think of absolutely nothing in life that is enhanced by a negative attitude, but a positive attitude can work wonders. It's an essential ingredient to success.

POSITIVE ATTITUDES DON'T LAST

Positive attitudes don't last? Is that true? Unfortunately it is. I've been reminded of this by people who choose to cling to a negative attitude because it's easier to maintain.

Of course I have a comeback for such a statement. Yes, a positive attitude won't last – but neither will a bath. You can't take a bath tonight and expect to remain clean forever. By the same token you can't develop a positive attitude today and expect it to carry you through life.

If we lived in a clean, sterile world, perhaps one bath per life would suffice, but this simply isn't the way it is. If we lived in a world devoid of pain and disappointment, perhaps we could develop a good attitude that would stay with us until death, but this simply isn't the way it is either.

Pain and disappointment occasionally will find you no matter where you are or what you do. It's simply a fact of life and such pain and disappointment can test your positive attitude. Just as we must take baths daily to keep ourselves clean, we must work on our attitudes regularly to keep them positive.

DIFFERENT TYPES OF ATTITUDES

Let's review the various types of attitudes a person may have, along with a brief description of each.

Negative.

This is simply the worst attitude anyone can have. This attitude will rob a person of happiness at each and every opportunity. Negative people about to take long trips may be convinced they'll die enroute to their destinations. When their children enroll in elementary school they may live in fear that they'll be abducted while they are outside playing or waiting for the school bus. To put it simply, a person with a negative attitude will find a reason not to enjoy anything good that may happen to him or her because he or she will look on the dark side of everything. Furthermore, a negative person generally won't undertake anything that might better his or her situation because he or she will dwell on the worst-case scenario that might arise from such an undertaking. For example, "I'm not going to put forth extra effort on the job because no one will notice and I'll be wasting my time." Another example? "I'm not going to invest my money because I'll probably lose it." Another example is, "Why make friends? They'll only stab you in the back." If you know such a person (hopefully, you aren't one yourself), don't look to him or her for humor; generally, they don't know the meaning of the word. People like this could stand a good mental bath to clean up their attitudes.

Unrealistic.

A person who has an unrealistic attitude is naive. Such a person initially believes it possible to lose 50 pounds in six weeks and stay healthy. Upon discovering the unhealthy truth, they become disillusioned and the unrealistic attitude often disappears. At this point the person's attitude could go either way. A negative attitude could develop because the person might be discouraged by the failure to achieve the unrealistic goal. On the other hand the person may develop a positive attitude because he or she now knows precisely the extent of effort needed to achieve the goal and is willing to pay the price.

Positive.

This is what we need to succeed. It isn't a "Pollyanna" type outlook; but it also isn't the awful attitude of a negative person. This is a realistic attitude that most successful people possess. The person with a positive attitude can laugh at himself or herself. Although such people might take their jobs most seriously, they don't take themselves seriously at all. They strive for excellent performances, but they don't react badly to criticism because they know that they must be their own best critics, and that constructive criticism is the route to personal and professional growth. They're willing to change when circumstances require a personal change because they're realistic enough to know that only they can change their lives for the better. They also know that by refusing to change, their personal situations might suffer. To paraphrase a famous saying, realistic people cope with the things in life that they can't change and work to change the things that they can. Furthermore, they can distinguish between the two.

I hope your attitude is positive. If it is, you'll find it easier to be successful. If your attitude is unrealistic or negative, why not make an effort to change?

CURTAIN UP

Some days just don't go well. Events beyond your control can get next to you. Even though you know you should react positively, it's difficult to do so. When people smile at you you feel like snarling. If someone asks you how you are you feel like telling them – in no uncertain terms!

In other words, your inside is sick. Perhaps it's only temporary and you know that after the day is over and you've had a good night's sleep you'll be fine. In the meantime, however, you must cope. And a bad attitude, even for only an hour, can cause you a week's worth of trouble if you alienate the wrong person or, worse yet, people.

I think a person who hides a negative attitude is actually considerate of others, much like a person with a communicable disease is considerate by taking every precaution to prevent its spread.

What do you do? Pretend you're an actor on stage and the curtain has just risen. You're playing the part of a person with a good attitude and take it from there.

When your inside is sick, you should decorate your outside. Is this deceitful? I know someone who thinks that it is. He believes that a person should let his or her true feelings show, no matter what the feelings are. To do otherwise, he says, is hypocritical.

I say that it's neither hypocritical nor deceitful. In fact, I think a person who hides a negative attitude is actually considerate of others, much like a person with a communicable disease is considerate by taking every precaution to prevent its spread. After all, a bad attitude is contagious (so is a good attitude for that matter, but I don't consider a good attitude a disease).

But there's a reason beyond being considerate for decorating your outside when your inside is sick. It's a positive reaction to a negative situation. Psychologists have long contended that it is easier to act your way into feeling than it is to feel your way into acting. To react with negative behavior to your negative moods just makes matters worse.

In other words, if you suffer from a negative attitude and you act accordingly you'll be feeding your negative attitude, which will get stronger (remember, the one you feed is the one that leads). On the other hand, if you choose to act as if you were motivated by a good attitude, although at the time you actually aren't, you may discover that soon, your bad attitude will give way to a good one.

In short, you can feel any way you'd like if you're willing to act that way. A University of California study showed that volunteers who feigned looks of fear actually responded physiologically as if they were actually afraid. Their heart rates accelerated and their skin temperatures decreased. When the volunteers acted angry, heart rates again increased along with their skin temperatures. When they looked disgusted, both heart rates and skin temperatures dropped. The conclusions of the study indicate that you can actually feel the way you wish you felt by acting the part.

I practiced this quite often to win time off from guard duty when I was stationed at Fort Ord military base in Monterey, California, in 1962. The selection of soldiers for guard duty was conducted by having all soldiers fall in for assembly.

Each soldier was to repeat his general orders to the officer in charge. As a matter of policy the outstanding soldier was exempt from guard duty.

I would get in front of the line-up, stand erect and look directly into the eye of the officer and repeat my general orders, looking and acting as confident as I could. More times than not, I found myself exempt from guard duty.

Did I actually feel confident? Not the first time I tried it. I didn't feel like I had any advantage over most of the other soldiers. After I saw that this practice would produce positive results, however, I found that I actually felt confident as I acted the part.

THINK POSITIVELY

Finally, there is another reason you should think and act positively – it's critical to success.

No matter what task you may face, a positive attitude will get you a lot farther than a negative one. A positive attitude won't necessarily guarantee that you'll succeed, but a negative attitude will virtually assure your failure.

Remember the story about The Little Steam Engine That Could? It started out believing that it couldn't climb a demanding hill. As a result, it couldn't. It climbed the hill with relative ease only after the steam engine developed a positive attitude. Instead of believing that it couldn't, it started to believe that it could, and that made the difference.

There are two types of people in the world – optimists and pessimists. Optimists don't always succeed, but they at least try. Therefore, they have a better chance of succeeding than pessimists who usually don't try at all and, therefore, can't succeed.

Many times it depends on how we look at a given situation. When I visited South Africa I toured Table Mountain, a massive rock with a flat top and a side that forms virtually a 90-degree angle with the earth. As I was going up in a cable car I wondered how anyone could climb to the top.

When I got out at the top I looked out over Cape Town, South Africa. The view was beautiful. I looked out over the back side and saw that the mountain descended gradually to the bottom, sporting beautiful green grass that could easily be walked upon. This mountain would be most difficult to climb from one side; from the other it would be a piece of cake.

Whenever we're faced with a "mountain" that we must "climb," we should always look at both sides to find the easiest way to get to the top.

The same is true at the Cape of Good Hope where the Atlantic and the Indian oceans merge. The Atlantic side is rough and cold, not a place where you would want to go swimming. Yet, the Indian Ocean is smooth and warm. Those who only look at the rough side would be needlessly discouraged if they wanted to take a dip.

ATTITUDE MAKES THE DIFFERENCE

Let me give you an example of the difference an attitude can make. There is an old legend that goes like this: two railroad employees in charge of inspecting and locking all freight cars were in the midst of their duties when one inadvertently locked the other in a refrigerated boxcar.

The man trapped inside called for help, but no one could hear him. Frantically, he began to write messages on the wall of the boxcar, indicating he knew that his life was in jeopardy. His final message indicated that he was only moments from death because he was falling victim to the refrigeration. If help wasn't forthcoming, his message stated, he would surely freeze to death.

The next day he was found, he was indeed dead, but he wasn't frozen. The refrigeration motor was out of commission and had been since before the previous night. The temperature in the boxcar had fallen no lower than 50 degrees – possibly an uncomfortable temperature but certainly not life-threatening.

The man had died only because he had made up his mind he would die. Had he been optimistic, he might have walked away with nothing more than a bad cold, if even that!

It may just be a legend, but there is truth in it. Though there may be limits on both ends to the power of thinking (a person can't will themselves into unaided flight just by believing it, and maybe a person can't die just by believing death is imminent), it doesn't change the truth that there is power in the attitude you maintain.

Be optimistic. Whatever job, task or dilemma you might face, think and act positively. Tell yourself you can succeed and give it your best effort. By doing so, you'll be in the best position for success. If you fail, at least you'll know you gave it your best effort. Furthermore, you'll perhaps learn some lessons that might help you succeed on your next attempt.

The pessimist will have nothing except possible regrets for not having tried, and too many regrets can drive you insane.

TAKE CARE OF YOUR ATTITUDE

Just as worry can undermine a person's belief system, it can also destroy a good attitude. It's hard to think and act positively when you're expecting the worst.

Would you be able to have a good attitude if you were

paralyzed for life? I recently saw someone who was confined to a wheelchair who obviously had a good attitude. On the back of the wheelchair was a bumper sticker that read, "I'd rather be dancing." He obviously used humor as a way of coping. After all, it's better to laugh about a bad situation than to cry.

Folk music legend Doc Watson is blind, but he doesn't let that interfere with his sense of humor. He once joked at a public performance that he went into a country store, picked up his seeing-eye dog by the tail and swung the animal around and around over his head. When the store clerk asked what he was doing, Watson replied, "Just looking around."

All of these people obviously like themselves, because their humor is self-directed. He chooses to believe that being blind only makes him different, not handicapped.

The other day, I saw a dilapidated car with a bumper sticker that read, "Answer my prayers; steal this car." The owner obviously could laugh at the fact that he or she didn't have a lot, materially speaking.

Worry is wasted energy that can cripple a belief system. If you worry about something you can change, don't worry and start changing. If it's something out of your control, then don't worry. Odds are good the dreaded expectation will never occur. Even if it does, worrying isn't going to help matters one way or the other.

Instead of spending good energy worrying, do something productive instead. You'll be better off.

LET YOUR ATTITUDE SHINE

Let me close this chapter with a final example. Do you think you could have a good attitude shining shoes for a living? If you said yes, great! If you said no, you obviously haven't met Tamara Brewer, an attractive young lady from Tulsa, Oklahoma, who shines shoes at one of the area hotels. I met her in January 1985 while conducting a collections seminar in Tulsa.

Tamara was pleasant and spoke to everyone who came by. I wanted to find out more about this woman so I sat for a shoeshine. Tamara, who was in her mid-twenties then, had worked for the state of Oklahoma in the tax department for three years. She quit a job that offered a good salary, a retirement program, sick pay and vacation benefits because she burned out from dealing with upset people, she said. She was never trained to deal with irate taxpayers. Oklahoma had no shortage of these because taxes had recently been raised, she said. As a result, she had come to dread the thought of going to work every morning.

She loved her new job, she said, looking forward to coming to work every day because she deals with nice people. Furthermore, she said she shines about 45 pairs of shoes each day. At $3.00 each, that amounts to $135.00. Add to that about $45.00 in tips, and she was making about $180.00 per day, or $900.00 per week. Multiply that times 50 weeks and she was making somewhere around $45,000 per year just shining shoes. Even if her workload were cut in half, she could still have drawn $22,500 annually – not a bad income at all.

Think you could get a good attitude about that? I know doctors and lawyers who don't make that much. Of course, virtually anyone could get a good attitude about a low-responsibility job that paid $45,000 per year. In Tamara's case, however, her income resulted from her good attitude, not vice versa. Her personal magnetism generated much of her business; without it, she'd be just another shoe shiner.

Good attitude makes the difference in every job – yours included. So does personal appearance. In fact, I didn't know anything about Tamara's attitude until I met her. Which was about the main reason why I noticed her.

There were other reasons why I noticed her. First, even before I noticed her attitude, was the fact that her appearance was immaculate; one would never know she shined shoes for a living unless he or she caught her in the act, which I did. Had she looked like many shoe shiners I've seen I wouldn't have paid her a second thought.

So, in addition to attitude, appearance is also important. In fact, the next chapter will be devoted to just this subject.

CHAPTER SUMMARY

❖ We can't control everything that happens to us, but we most certainly can control our reaction to events that affect us. When we can do that, our attitude is under control.

❖ Anyone can have a good attitude, regardless of their situation. Many times, a person's lot in life is determined by his or her attitude.

❖ Just as we must take baths daily to keep ourselves clean, we must work on our attitudes regularly to keep them positive.

❖ There are three different types of attitudes a person can have negative, unrealistic and positive. A positive attitude is essential for success.

❖ Decorate your outside when your inside is sick. You can actually feel the way you wish you felt by acting the part.

❖ There are two types of people in the world – optimists and pessimists. Optimists don't always succeed, but they at least try. Therefore, they have a better chance of succeeding than pessimists, who usually don't try at all and, therefore, can't succeed.

❖ It's hard to think and act positively when you're expecting the worst.

CHAPTER NINE

Look Sharp, Feel Sharp, Be Sharp!

Some people think clothes don't make a difference!

There is a funny illustration with the theme that is identical to its title, which is Clothes Make The Man. It is the story of three thieves, one of whom was large and domineering in physical stature but who, as far as criminal intent was concerned, was more or less along for the ride.

The mastermind of the trio hatched a plot that would make them rich, he said. He and the second man could rob houses at will. If they were caught, their large accomplice, clad in police uniform, could "arrest" them. Of course, instead of taking them back to jail, they would go back to their hideout with the evidence.

It seemed like such a grand plan until they tried it. The

large man posing as a police officer was stationed outside a home that the other two were burglarizing. While standing guard, he was greeted by several passing citizens who, taking him for a police officer, treated him with appropriate respect. When the two thieves had finished ransacking the house and were escaping with the loot, they were "arrested" by their accomplice, who held them back until the real police arrived.

The two thieves learned the hard way that clothes indeed can have a strong influence on the way a person is not only perceived, but on the way he or she actually behaves.

The same can be said for appearance in general. A person's sense of self-worth is bound to be affected by the manner in which the person presents himself or herself. By the same token, the reverse is also true. The way a person presents himself or herself is a reflection of that person's sense of self-worth.

GOOD APPEARANCE IS VITAL TO SUCCESS

I don't care what a person does for a living, his or her success will at worst hinge on personal appearance and, at best, could be increased by improved personal appearance. This is true even if you're in a dirty business. A neat, well groomed garbage collector is going to get more respect than one who looks like he spent the night in a dumpster.

Appearance is the most important factor of any first impression. Upon seeing us for the first time people don't necessarily know how good or bad our attitudes are, but they can certainly guess by the way we look. If you meet a person who has twelve inches of bright green hair sticking up from the top of their head you can easily guess that that person might have something to say about "society." I am not saying the person is bad for having green hair, but I am saying that the appearance tells us something. In this case it is a person who knows they are making a statement. The problem is when a person is unaware that their attitude and their values are on display in the way they appear.

A bad attitude is likely to show itself in a person's appearance as well as his or her facial and verbal expressions.

Recent studies show that 55 percent of the impact we have on people is determined by physical appearance. This is the reason we should dress for the position we want to obtain, provided it is not one where a uniform is required. In other words our appearance should reflect our goals.

Some people think appearance isn't important, yet they would be upset if some professional people didn't place any importance on their appearances. For example, uniforms reflect authority, concern and credibility. Some examples of jobs where uniforms are critical to delivering an appropriate image include police officers, firefighters and airline pilots. A person who needs a police officer for protection might not feel secure with one who was clad in bermuda shorts, sandals and a T-shirt.

Let's take airline pilots as an example. If you think appearance isn't important, how would you feel if you were seated inside a plane and in walked the pilot – sporting faded jeans, dirty hair, a haggard face, an overnight beard growth, and bloodshot eyes. Would you feel good about flying?

Suppose instead another pilot entered the plane. Suppose this pilot was well groomed and dressed in a clean, neatly pressed uniform. Suppose he had good posture and a face that reflected confidence and enthusiasm. Which pilot would you rather have at the controls?

Actually, the first pilot might have been the more experienced and competent pilot who, because of lost luggage and perhaps a sick child at home, might have let his appearance slide. Although his bad appearance shouldn't affect his skills as a pilot, we wouldn't feel comfortable because of his appearance.

As unfair as that might sound, it's a fact of life. Successful people accept it.

DRESS PROPERLY

I'll never forget the day I learned just how important it is that we "dress for success," if I may borrow that phrase from best-selling author Jim Malloy. I was attending a National Speakers Association session when the featured speaker asked us to determine the line of business of the person sitting next to us, judging by his or her clothes.

The man sitting beside me immediately started apologizing for his state of dress; as far as I could see, he was the only person present who wasn't wearing a suit. Obviously he felt that his casual attire wasn't in keeping with his professional image. The more he apologized the more embarrassed I felt for him. I've never forgotten that, and I doubt I ever will.

Although it has been said that people shouldn't judge others by the way they dress, people often do, especially in business situations. Therefore, it's important to let your state of dress reflect a positive image on yourself and your line of work.

In the business world it's best to dress conservatively. In fact, it has been said that a person should dress to satisfy his or her most conservative client of the day. A client who appreciates modern styles will forgive a conservative dresser much more willingly than a conservative client will forgive a "faddish" dresser.

Of course, if your job involves a uniform, you don't have

to worry about selecting proper attire. However, you should still be concerned with the way you present yourself. A dirty, wrinkled uniform says a lot about the person wearing it, and none of it is good.

If your job has a dress code, follow it. If you're in charge of establishing a dress code, solicit input from your staff. If your state of attire is left open, dress for your situation at worst! For best results, dress for the role you would like to play in your career. For example, if you desire to be in management, dress like a manager. This strategy helped elevate me to management status when I worked for General Finance Company's largest consumer loan office prior to starting American Accounts Collection Agency, Inc.

You're always being observed. Therefore, you shouldn't lose credibility because of the way you dress.

QUALITY COUNTS!

Did you hear the joke about the man who went to Brooks Brothers and asked the salesman to show him a cheap suit? The salesman told the customer to look in the mirror.

When buying clothes, don't sacrifice quality for quantity. Certainly you can't afford to buy clothes that are out of your budget, but on the other hand you can't afford to sacrifice quality. First, quality clothes last longer and, therefore, give you greater value. Second, better quality makes a better impression and as a result makes you more easily remembered. This can be critical to your success.

By the same token, an inferior suit can make you remembered, too. Consider the man who went to a business convention where he saw a woman he had met the previous year. He approached the woman an asked her if she remembered him, to which she replied, "Indeed, I do. I'd recognize that suit anywhere."

Wear quality clothes. If you have a limited budget, simply buy fewer clothes. Quality counts.

FINISHING TOUCHES

Dress is important, but don't forget that making a good appearance requires a 100 percent effort. A sharp looking suit will stand out like a sore thumb if the rest of you looks like you should be digging a ditch. Let's review the finishing touches to making a good appearance.

Hair.

Length depends on standards set by your career, although long hair for men for the most part is unacceptable by today's standards; for the most part, it should not touch a man's collar. In any event, it should be clean and well groomed, preferably in conservative to moderate fashion. Specialty cuts, such as spiked hair, Mohawks and crew cuts (especially for women) probably wouldn't be appropriate for business. Women have a variety of styles from which they may choose, but men and women should remember that their hair should compliment their appearance, not distract from it.

Nails.

For men, they should be short. For women, they should be kept a tasteful length – the shorter, the better. Like hair, they should not distract from a person's appearance. In any event, they should be kept clean.

Teeth.

This one is easy for both sexes. They should be kept clean by regular brushing and flossing. This practice not only cleans the teeth, but also helps to eliminate bad breath and the potential for gum disease.

Shoes.

Conservative laced shoes or loafers are appropriate for business situations. Women have a broader variety from which to choose. In any event, they should be kept clean and polished.

Don't let your appearance suffer by sins of omission. Don't forget to take care of the finishing touches when preparing your appearance.

TAKE CARE OF YOUR ENVIRONMENT

Just how good of a first impression will you be able to make if your car looks like a garbage can on wheels? I once hired a manager for American Accounts. He took me to lunch one day in his car. After I got inside, I was sorry we hadn't taken mine.

I'm not saying that his car was dirty, although indeed it was. I'm not saying that his car was filthy, although it easily qualified for that status. This man's car was simply foul! I was embarrassed; he wasn't. He seemed to be right at home. Fortunately we didn't go to a drive-in hamburger stand to eat in the car. I would have never been able to stomach it. (Incidentally, the manager is no longer with us).

There's a good reason for the origin of the saying, "You can tell a lot about a person by looking at his or her car." It's true. A person with no pride in his or her car very well might lack pride in other things, too.

The same can be said about your home. You may look as

fresh and crisp as a new dollar bill, but if your home looks like a pig's sty, people will judge you. Sad, but true.

Of course, your boss may not ever see your home, but he or she will see your desk at work. If you aspire to a position that requires organization, don't let your desk disqualify you from consideration.

Perhaps you're not one to leave half-filled cups of coffee and partially eaten sweet rolls on your desktop until they're taken over by mold and/or ants. Keeping your desk clean, however, isn't enough. In the real world, a clean and neat environment is impressive.

For example, while traveling through Europe, I was amazed at the differences in the various countries. Many of the countries I visited were dirty and their public facilities were health hazards. On the other hand, I was especially impressed by the pride the Germans take in the appearance of their country. They work together to keep it clean. Their public restrooms, streets and transportation stations are clean and devoid of offensive odors.

The appearance of a country can make you feel either safe and secure or fearful and uneasy. As a result, which country do you think I am planning to revisit?

Keep your environment clean, neat and organized. If you don't, you might make the wrong impression at the wrong time.

YOUR BODY TALKS!

Your body itself will tell people a lot about you. If you're not clean, your body will tell people that you need a bath.

Of course, that's just the beginning of the story. Your body also will tell people what you think of yourself and the world around you. If you're accustomed to slouching, you'll give not only the impression that you've been beaten down by the world, but also that you no longer care what impression you make on others. This isn't in your best interests in any situation, especially one that may lead to career advancement.

Body language often says more than a person's words. Just the way a person stands can tell you much about him or her. For example, I found it interesting to watch President Ronald Reagan and Vice President George Bush share a podium. Reagan took up almost twice as much space as Bush, and it's not because Reagan was almost twice as big as Bush. Instead, Reagan stood with his feet apart, his shoulders back and his body erect. He let his posture reflect the importance of his position by taking up as much space as comfortably possible.

> Though body language may in actuality have little to do with a person's competence, it does have a lot to do witth a person's confidence!

On the other hand, Bush tended to stand with his feet together, his shoulders forward and his arms close to his side. Unlike Reagan, he tended to take up as little space as possible.

Though body language may in actuality have little to do with a person's competence, it does have a lot to do with a person's confidence! Remember, it's easier to act your way into feeling than it is to feel your way into acting. And Reagan, being a former actor, probably knew this better than Bush.

He undoubtedly learned about posture and body language during his years as an actor and was smart enough to carry it over into the real world.

The fact that Bush didn't have a powerful physical stance when next to Regan was clearly not a reflection of either his confidence or competence. He did become the 41st President of the United States. However, suppose you had two men applying for the same job that required a person with confidence and competence. One held himself like Reagan, the other held himself like Bush. All things being equal, who would you hire?

Stand tall and erect. Slouching can add to painful back problems, so not only will you look and feel more confident, your body will actually be better for it.

YOUR EYES TELL THE TRUTH

Even if your appearance is immaculate and your posture indicates confidence, your eyes can give you away. What's the old saying, the eyes are the window on the soul?

Or as the French say "The eyes are the mirror of the soul" ("Les yeux sont le miroir de l'dme").

In any phase of life eye contact is essential. A person who can't look another in the eye usually is uncomfortable about something. If you can't make eye contact with someone, the person with whom you're talking might wonder if you're being honest. On the other hand, the person might doubt your self-confidence and competence. Regardless of the situation, the other person's impression of you likely won't be favorable.

Good eye contact doesn't mean staring down another person. Effective eye contact involves looking at another person's eyes for about three to six seconds. Prolonged eye contact often is a sign of aggression, which a member of the opposite sex might interpret as sexually oriented. If you're about to ask someone for a date, prolonged eye contact might be a good tactic, depending on the person. For business purposes however, prolonged eye contact might create discomfort.

Your appearance and body language is often just as important as your attitude, mainly because if people dismiss you on the basis of your appearance they'll never know how good an attitude you may have. There are few things in life that a person is able to control, so he or she might as well control these: attitude and appearance.

> **Staying in charge of your attitude, appearance and actions can be the ulti-imate way to create good first impressions.**

Of course, a person should also be in control of his or her actions. This is the third element of the triangle of the things within your control. Staying in charge of your attitude, appearance and actions can be the ultimate in creating good first impressions. Let me explain.

In Tokyo all taxicab drivers wear white gloves and drive immaculately clean cabs. Although I do not speak Japanese I nevertheless reached my destination each time I needed to go somewhere because the cab drivers were as helpful as they were courteous. In fact, they were insulted if you offered them tips. They consider themselves ambassadors for their country. They make you feel safe.

Compare this situation to what is often found in metropolitan U.S. cities where the cabs are commonly unclean, the driver mumbles to you, refuses to help you with your luggage, gets lost twice (possibly on purpose) and makes you pay for his or her mistakes. Such lack of consideration, if not outright incompetence, can ruin your entire trip (can you tell I've had lots of less than desirable cab rides in my home country?).

Recently I was in Cleveland, Ohio, where I had the opportunity to patronize a cab company called Americab. The company guarantees you a clean cab, courteous driver, and a fair price. This is the company I'll call the next time I'm in Cleveland.

Stay in charge of your actions. This is a broad topic in itself that involves far more than just your conduct. Turn to the next chapter and I'll explain.

CHAPTER SUMMARY

❖ A person's appearance can have strong influence on the way he or she not only is perceived, but on the way he or she actually behaves.

❖ A person's success will at worst hinge on personal appearance and, at best, could be increased by improved personal appearance.

❖ Appearance is the most important factor of any first impression. Recent studies show that 55 percent of the impact we have on people is determined by physical appearance. One meeting with someone is the only chance a person sometimes gets, so make use of every tool to leave the person wanting to meet you again.

❖ In the business world, it's best to dress conservatively. Dress for the role you would like to play in your career. For example, if you desire to be in management, dress like a manager.

❖ When buying clothes, don't sacrifice quality for quantity. Quality clothes give you greater value. Plus, better quality makes a better impression, which can be critical to your success.

❖ Don't overlook the finishing touches – hair, nails, teeth and shoes when preparing your appearance. You don't have to over-do it with gawdy styles and alarming colors, but it is important to remember the little things that help to leave a good impression.

❖ People also will judge you by the appearance of your environment your home, automobile and office.

❖ Posture also plays an important role in appearance. Body language often says more than a person's chosen words.

❖ Eye contact is essential for making a good first impression. Don't avoid it, but don't prolong it, either. Eye contact for three to six seconds at a time makes a good impression in the business world.

CHAPTER TEN

Stay In Charge

Some Americans thrive on action. Statistics will bear this out. On an average day, Americans eat 47 million hot dogs, drink 23 million gallons of soft drinks and spend $300 million on clothes. In the United States on any given day, joggers log 28 million miles, 200 people become millionaires, 800,000 people board passenger planes and 110 golfers score holes-in-one.

Then there's the down side. Aches and pains prompt Americans to swallow 52 tons of aspirin daily. One out of every six Americans regularly depend on some form of tranquilizer. At least 38 million Americans suffer from high blood pressure, and only a minority have it under control.

Cardiovascular disease is responsible for nearly one million deaths per year. According to the American Heart Association, 869,724 people died as the result of heart disease in the United States in 2004. Startlingly, the AHA says 16 million are living with heart disease. Unless statistics change, this means there is a good chance that when it comes your time to go, heart disease will be your calling card for entry into the next life.

What is causing this? Is it stress? Not exactly. Instead it's people's actions in response to stress that will cause the problem. Let me explain.

A STRESSFUL SOCIETY

We live in a stressful society. Life's pressures are extreme. Expenses mount, personal problems develop, worry ensues and performance suffers. Escape is often sought through nicotine, alcohol, drugs or excessive calories. As a result people gain weight and health problems mount, they lose pride and confidence, stop caring and then die. This death isn't necessarily physical; sometimes, they hang around for thirty or forty years before they're buried!

In short, they've lost control. They've allowed themselves to be beaten by the stress they've created in response to circumstances. The result often is burnout and resignation to what no longer satisfies them, be it a job situation, home life or both.

That's a lousy way to live, because a person who accepts such a situation is, in effect, admitting that he or she has lost control of his or her life.

It needn't be that way. And it would stop being that way if these people would take charge of their lives by taking control of their actions – and reactions.

ACT RESPONSIBLY

People often say they don't have sufficient time to achieve their goals. Yet, studies show that the average American spends more than 4 hours a day watching a television. That's by the A.C. Neilson Co. Others put the number as high as 7 hours per day. That's between 28 and 50 hours per week – on the high end it is ten hours more than most people put in on their jobs! On the low end it still adds up. Twenty-eight hours is more than one full day a week spent in front of a colorful, talking box.

> Most people have plenty of time to reach their goals. Their problem is that they have never prioritized their lives.

Perhaps you don't watch television, or at least you don't watch it seven hours daily. Is there anything else that you do that involves time that could be put to better use?

Most people have plenty of time to reach their goals. Their problem is the fact that they have never prioritized their lives.

There's an old rule that's applicable to virtually every phase of life. It applies with equal force to the work place as well as the home front. It's called the Pareto Principle, and it states that only 20 percent of a person's efforts produce 80 percent of positive results. Unfortunately, this also means that the remaining 80 percent of a person's efforts will achieve only 20 percent of positive results. What a waste!

Take a good look at your life to determine if this applies

to you. If it does, think of the increased positive results you could achieve by prioritizing your life.

The system is simple. After you've formed your list of goals, you'll know what you must do to achieve them. On a daily basis, you should write down the most important things you must do to achieve your goals. Then follow the list like a road map. Complete the most important task before you proceed to the second-most important task, and complete that one before moving on to the next item.

Sound too simple to be true? It will work if you take this seriously. Unfortunately, it doesn't work for many people because they won't take it seriously. Instead, they're sidetracked by their own bad habits.

HABITS CAN MAKE OR BREAK YOU

If you were to make a "to do" list based not on what you intend to do in a week, but what you actually do in a week, what would this list look like?

I've never known anyone to make a daily priority list that read like the following list: Watch five hours of television today, smoke two packs of cigarettes, overeat at every meal, and down a pint of bourbon.

Yet, I have known people who would have lists just like that if the lists conformed with their lifestyles. In other words, they don't have time to achieve their goals because their bad habits are keeping them too busy.

Bad habits are easy to develop and hard to live with, while good habits are hard to develop and easy to live with. As noted author Somerset Maugham said, "The unfortunate thing about this world is that good habits are so much easier to give up than bad ones."

You've undoubtedly heard the expression, "The road to

hell is paved with good intentions." Many people intend to do well with their lives, but their bad habits get in their way. Let's review several bad habits that tend to be obstacles to people's goals.

Lack of Exercise.

Good exercise habits are probably the best prevention against cardiovascular disease; bad exercise habits are probably one of the leading contributors. Regular exercise builds muscle, stimulates and strengthens the heart, prevents clogging of arteries, increases stamina and lung power and simply adds years to a lifetime in general.

Of course, a person who doesn't exercise enjoys none of these benefits. As a result, the body in general will be more susceptible to illness and disease. Add to that the fact that a person with decreased muscle tone will burn fewer calories than a person with good muscle tone. Therefore, the person with decreased muscle tone won't be able to eat as much as a person with a well developed body.

Poor Diet.

A proper diet will do much to add years to a person's life. Three square meals derived from the four basic food groups – meat, fish and poultry, dairy products, fruits and vegetables and grains – will provide sufficient fiber, nutrients and vitamins to keep the body operating efficiently, effectively and – most of all – energetically.

On the other hand, a person who regularly skips breakfast, frequently lunches on fast food and may or may not have a good healthy dinner might find himself or herself sluggish, if not physically ill, in little time at all. You are what you eat.

Excesses.

Anything you do to excess isn't good. If too much of a good thing isn't good, then too much of a not-so-good thing can be terrible. I used to smoke three packs of cigarettes per day, but I dropped the habit after realizing it was something I couldn't live with. It's best to drink in moderation or not to drink alcohol at all. Although I know many successful people who drink, most if not all of them, moderate their drinking. I still enjoy occasional desserts and sweets, but I've had to learn to practice moderation with those, too. If you're doing anything excessively, you've probably got a problem that you need to deal with. Otherwise, the excess may deal with you unfavorably.

I know what I'm talking about. At the age of 35, I weighed 198 pounds. Considering I stand five-feet, seven-inches tall, this was more weight than I could comfortably handle. It took proper diet and a lot of exercise to lose more than 40 pounds. It wasn't easy, but it was worth the effort. I now maintain a weight of about 155 pounds – seven pounds less than I weighed when I was discharged from the service in the mid 1960s.

Procrastination.

This is indeed a bad habit, practiced by virtually all of us at one time or another. Home or office projects are put off indefinitely, although the original intent was to "do it tomorrow." Procrastinators find that tomorrow never comes. They're also frustrated people, for the most part.

Wasting Time.

This one can cost us plenty if we do it often enough. People who use their time wisely usually get good results;

people who don't use their time wisely usually get inferior results. Learn to use time more efficiently. Here's how.

Budget your time. You've heard it said that time is money. I say that time is more important than money. If you lose a dollar, you can earn another. If you lose an hour, you've lost it. Once elapsed, it's irretrievable.

Time is one thing that makes us all equal. Rich and poor, saint and sinner alike have the same amount. It's how they use it that counts.

For example, if I gave you $168 at the beginning of each week you could build yourself a substantial financial nest egg by saving all or a portion of each deposit I made in your account.

Suppose instead I gave you 168 hours at the beginning of each week. By the time the beginning of next week rolled around, you'd be out of time and needing some more. There are only 168 hours per week, and all of us spend time at the same rate. Unlike money, it can't be saved; you can put it to good use, or you can waste it. The choice is yours.

Take your priority list and assign a reasonable amount of time for each task, then schedule it into your day.

Use Down Time. Don't get caught in a position where you're forced to waste time. Keep paperwork handy when your flight is delayed; or read a book. Put a CD player or ipod in your car and listen to audio recordings. All types of learning and motivational programs are available. Studies show that the average worker spends 64 minutes each day commuting to and from work. That's five hours and 20 minutes per week of instruction that you could get during time that you might ordinarily be listening to the radio or doing nothing but driving.

Lethargy.

Some people feel too tired at the end of a work day to do anything but plop themselves down in front of the television for 7 hours. Perhaps their tiredness results from poor nutrition or lack of exercise. If not, perhaps the problem and the solution lies in the law of inertia.

This law states that an object in motion tends to remain in motion, while an object at rest tends to remain at rest. It takes far less energy to get started and remain in operation than it does to start and stop frequently throughout the day.

Make the law of inertia work for you instead of against you. Make even the break times you take during the day a matter for re-energizing your work and not for putting off important duties. At home, pass up the television or some other non-productive activity for a stimulating project that will lead you closer to your goals.

Don't let these bad habits interfere with your journey to success. If you don't have these bad habits, don't develop them. If you do, work at eliminating them. When you do, you'll have more time and energy to devote to the pursuit of your goals.

WATCH YOURSELF IN PUBLIC

Why is behavior important to success? Simple. It's not so much that you'll be noticed for good behavior, although that is indeed possible. Your behavior is important because if you don't behave, you will definitely be noticed.

A man I know was on a business trip and happened to stay at the same hotel as a national celebrity, whose name won't be mentioned. To make a long story short, the celebrity was dissatisfied with the service he was receiving in the hotel restaurant and was sounding off in not-so-polite terms. The cursing seemed to get worse as the evening progressed, according to my friend.

Needless to say, my friend's opinion of this celebrity was considerably lessened after that evening. When the celebrity's name is mentioned, my friend doesn't think of the successful weekly comedy series this celebrity used to have. Instead, he thinks of the night in the restaurant when the celebrity acted like a horse's posterior.

Perhaps the celebrity had received rotten service indeed, but that's no excuse. We can't always control what happens to us, but we most certainly can control our reactions to occurrences that affect us. When we don't control our reactions, we tend to behave badly, and this story just goes to show that we're remembered most when we're at our worst.

Our actions will tell on us. They're a vital part of our lives. People don't get into trouble at work as much as they get into trouble after work. I know of a salesman who staged an excellent presentation and was on the verge of landing a large contract. Before the deal was closed the salesman and his prospects went out to dinner at a local restaurant where the salesperson proceeded to get smashed. His professional behavior gave way to obnoxiousness and belligerence; needless to say there was no sale.

Our actions will help determine our success or failure. A person isn't likely to rise within any organization if he or she tends to be an embarrassment to management, regardless of whether his or her bad behavior occurs on or off company time.

Furthermore, we've got to remember that we're always role models to someone, whether it be a child, a new employee or just a friend. We must practice what we preach. A father can tell his children how they should behave, but if he really wants to get his message across, he had best serve as a good example. People would rather see a sermon than hear one any day.

To sum it up, your actions will take you either closer to or farther away from your goals, depending on what they are. Stay in control. If you haven't already, take charge of your actions. When you're in charge of your actions, you'll also find it easy to take charge of your people skills. I'll explain in the next chapter.

CHAPTER SUMMARY

❖ It isn't stress that ruins people's health, but it is their actions in response to stress that adversely affects them. Successful people are in control of their actions.

❖ Most people have plenty of time to reach their goals. Their problem is the fact that they have never prioritized their lives.

❖ Bad habits are easy to obtain and hard to live with, while good habits are hard to develop and easy to live with. Don't let bad habits interfere with your journey to success.

❖ Watch your behavior in public. If you don't, everyone else will. We're remembered most when we're at our worst.

❖ Our actions will help determine our success or failure. Take charge of them.

SECTION FOUR
People Skills

People skills: The ability to work well with others.

The Inukshuk are symbols of community. Though alone and constructed in barren places, inuksuit represent people working together to help one another. Their very construction often involves many hands. One use of the inuksuit in ancient times was for a small group of people to build a line of inuksuit to look like a line of people. Caribou would be chased toward the line. Suspecting the inuksuit were real people the caribou would turn and run in a direction where hunters waited in hiding. This is one of the many examples of the way a small group of people working together accomplish a lot. Ancient travelers knew they could not survive without community - they guarded their relationships and developed ways to make their relationships work for the common good.

CHAPTER ELEVEN

Be Nice or Be Sorry!

When you leave home for work, are the people you leave there happy to see you go? More importantly, are they sorry to see you return? If this is so, suffice it to say that your people skills just might leave something to be desired.

When you take breaks at work do you find others changing their breaks to a different time? If this is the case, perhaps your people skills are to blame. When you take your lunch hour do you find yourself watching to see where others go to lunch and then decide to eat elsewhere to avoid certain people? If so, perhaps their people skills are to blame. (Of course, some people begrudgingly go to lunch with a group of people they don't like. They join them because they know that someone in the group is going to rip someone else to shreds, and it very well might be them if they're not present to prevent it.)

On the whole people don't like to be around people with poor people skills. In a job situation, people may enjoy the work and working conditions. Yet, if they must work with too many people with poor people skills, they'll eventually find other jobs.

In more than 1,500 seminars I've conducted, I state that the three most important traits of a successful person are knowledge of product or services, technical skills and human relations skills. Then I would ask my audience which of the three traits was most important.

Without exception, the overwhelming majority of each audience voted for people skills – the ability to get along with others. When I asked them to be specific about what people skills involve they would most often include positive attitude, ability to listen well, a pleasing tone of voice, sympathy, empathy, good eye contact, and sincerity.

The people at these seminars were simply regular people who were trying to learn how to manage themselves better. In other words, they were pretty much representative of people we see in the work force every day. In defining people skills, these people were saying what they liked in others; the opposite of those traits (for example, negative attitude, offensive tone of voice, insensitivity, etc.) would be qualities that would turn them off.

In this age of progress, people skills are simply essential. While computers and other machines are rapidly taking over many people's jobs, good people skills will be your "ace in the hole," so to speak. With all the advancements of modern society, I feel safe in saying that the machine will never be invented that can function with good people skills. On the other hand, virtually any machine will be less offensive than (and, thus, favored over) a worker who possesses poor people skills

In short, your ability to get along with people can either make or break your career.

PEOPLE LIKE JOBS FOR DIFFERENT REASONS

A poll printed in USA Today indicated that seven out of ten adults work outside the home, and that 9 percent of them like their jobs. Of those who enjoy their jobs, 32 percent said they like the work itself; 23 percent said they like their co-workers; 12 percent said they like the money; 7 percent said they like the hours; 6 percent said they like the company benefits; 3 percent said they like the boss; 16 percent said there were other reasons; and 1 percent said they didn't know.

What I find interesting about the survey is that a total of 26 percent of the people enjoyed their jobs because they liked the people they work with – either their co-workers and/or their boss. These people didn't say they liked salary or working conditions, although they very well might have. They said that what they liked best about the job was the people.

It's important that people enjoy their careers to be happy, but it's also important that they can get along with their co-workers. If they can't, problems can develop.

GET ALONG WITH CUSTOMERS, TOO!

Let's look at another survey that was conducted to determine why people quit doing business with a particular person or establishment. The survey showed that 1 percent of former customers will never come back because they have died. 3 percent of ex-customers have moved away, and 5 percent have a friend in the business somewhere else. Nine percent of quitting customers have a complaint, and 14 percent are just dissatisfied with the product or service. The remaining 68 percent of customers who walk out of the establishment for the last time are alienated by the attitude of the business' staff!

This can have a tremendous impact on a businessperson mainly because he or she may never know why most of his or her customers are leaving. A White House study shows that 96 percent of unhappy customers never complain to business management.

It doesn't end there, however. On the average each dissatisfied customer will tell at least 9 other people and 13 percent of them will tell more than 20 people.

Can you afford to have unhappy customers? I can't. One way businesses can keep at least 68 percent of their customers (and possibly as many as 91 percent, counting those who had complaints or were dissatisfied with the product or service) is by making sure that their staff are trained at maintaining good relationships with their customers.

GOOD PEOPLE SKILLS ARE ESSENTIAL!

With the previous surveys in mind, I think it's safe to say that one reason people buy from certain salespeople is because they like them. That's not to say that product isn't important, because it is. Yet, the behavior and demeanor of the salesperson is equally important. Otherwise the customer would order by catalog.

I haven't seen any studies on why employers hire certain people and pass over others. Having been an employer at American Accounts I can tell you that I hired only people who had either good people skills or at least what I perceived to be good potential people skills. Very few people that I hired had good knowledge of our services, most of them having no experience in debt collection. Few if any possessed good technical skills, but I knew those traits could develop in time.

People skills are something entirely different. Yes, they can be developed, but people who need to develop such skills will have their work cut out for them. It isn't any more difficult to learn good people skills than it is to learn any other skill. However, people who lack these skills generally have attitude problems that tend to interfere with their ability to learn them.

I can think of no element of life where good people skills aren't beneficial. A person who tries to make friends without them will find little success. A person who tries to manage his or her family will be very much in need of people skills. It's essential for positive interaction with co-workers. Even a customer will find that he or she will receive better service by displaying good people skills.

SOME MANAGERS HAVE IT, SOME DON'T!

In a "Beetle Bailey" newspaper cartoon strip, Beetle was complaining to Sgt. Snorkel about the army. The sergeant replied, "Beetle, you have all the benefits of free room and board, transportation, medical care, on the job training, and you get paid for it. What more could you want?" Beetle replied, "Better management."

If the strip had continued for one more frame, the sergeant probably would have pounded Beetle into a pulp, as he frequently does. Beetle was actually saying that the sergeant could benefit by developing people skills.

Of course, managers (like military sergeants) must be task-oriented. A manager who places neither urgency nor importance on company goals and quotas will likely be looking for another job. Many managers like Sgt. Snorkel, however, make the mistake of thinking that task orientation alone is sufficient. Sooner or later they either develop bleeding ulcers or they learn they can't sufficiently motivate subordinates through task orientation alone.

> **Your ability to get along with people can either make or break your career.**

By the same token, people orientation is a good quality for any manager. However, if it's his or her only quality, there may be trouble. Although the manager might be well liked, he or she might not necessarily be respected.

The best managers are people/task oriented. Certainly, they hand out orders, but they also take the time to make sure their subordinates understand the orders and feel good about them.

SOME COMPANIES OBVIOUSLY DON'T CARE

It never ceases to amaze me how some companies don't seem to recognize the importance of teaching good people skills. Companies will spend millions of dollars developing their operations and advertising their products and/or services. Yet, customers are routinely alienated when a company representative doesn't know how (or, worse yet, doesn't care) to handle a real complaint.

Remember Tamara Brewer, the shoe-shine lady I mentioned in the chapter on attitudes? The State of Oklahoma's tax department lost a fine employee because no one taught her how to deal positively with irate taxpayers. With some people skill training, Tamara might have kept her job and proven to be a real asset to the department. As it was, she quit her job to shine shoes because she was tired of dealing with upset customers. (Of course, when I met her, Tamara was doing quite well shining shoes; she's a woman who knows how to turn a problem into an opportunity.)

A BAD EXPERIENCE

I had an experience with an airline company that I won't soon forget. Unless or until I do you can bet that the airline will get no more of my business. Preparing to leave Orlando, Florida, I arrived at the company's baggage check station 20 minutes prior to my flight's departure. Seventeen minutes later someone finally checked my luggage. That left me three minutes to catch my plane.

I arrived at the gate before the plane took off. There, I learned that I would not be on board when it did. Passengers who aren't at the gate at least 10 minutes prior to departure are considered no-shows, an attendant told me, and their seats are forfeited.

I didn't like that, but I could have lived with it. What actually angered me was the fact that absolutely no one employed by the airline showed me the least bit of sympathy. I tried to explain that the reason for my delay in arriving at the gate was because of the delay in getting my luggage checked. The gate attendant wasn't interested. "Sir," he said. "You weren't here 10 minutes before take-off. You lost your seat. If this causes you a problem, you'll have to work it out for yourself." In an attempt to find someone to assist me I returned to the baggage checking attendant. I explained to her that I lost my seat because of her delay in checking my luggage.

"It's not my fault," she said. "If you have a problem, you'll have to take it up with someone else."

I got back from Orlando, but it was on a different airline. Furthermore, there will be ice cream parlors in a place that's a lot hotter than Orlando in the summertime before I ever buy a ticket on that airline again. As far as I'm concerned, the money they spend on advertising is just thrown away.

A GREAT EXPERIENCE

On the other hand, there are many fine businesses and establishments that thrive because the employees have good people skills. I once spent a week at the Las Colinas Health Club in Dallas, Texas. A young woman by the name of Lee Ann Evans was my contact in the organization. I arrived late on a Saturday night; first thing Sunday morning Lee Ann called me to make sure I had arrived safely and to ask if I needed anything. That call let me know that there were people there who cared whether I arrived.

Shortly after the call, I needed some information, so I called the desk operator, who answered the phone saying, "Yes, Mr. Arnold, how may we help you?"

I was impressed not because the operator addressed me as "mister," but by the fact that she knew my name. People like to hear the sound of their own names from others, and I'm no exception. It's an important people skill.

Lee Ann and I met to review my schedule for the week. Lee Ann let me know that her job was to do what she could to make sure that I would have the best week I'd ever spent in my life at the health club. She found out all about my likes and dislikes by asking questions.

That's another important part of people skills. A person

who asks questions shows interest in the other person's situation. In fact, this is a basic rule for salespeople. Selling is not a telling business. The salesperson who spends all of his or her time telling a prospect what a wonderful product or service he or she sells runs the risk of boring the prospect to death. The same principle is involved in making friends; spend all your time talking about how great you are and the person you're talking with may decide that you're not so great at all.

It's like the old saying goes, "People don't care how much you know, unless they know how much you care." It's true virtually in any and every phase of life. Many talented people in all kinds of professions have learned this lesson the hard way.

> I shouldn't have to give you advice on how to employ good people skills with people you like. It should come naturally. It's the people you don't like that may give you trouble.

Finally, Lee Ann checked with me every day to make sure that my needs and comforts were being met. She was truly concerned about how much I was enjoying my stay and wanted to do everything she could to make it better.

In a nutshell, to serve people's needs to the best of your ability is a good people skill. I go to certain restaurants not only because I like the food, but because I like the people who serve me. I've found through the years that I'll make far more concessions for mistakes and errors from people who are kind, considerate and conscientious than I'll grant for those who act like I'm a problem that they wish would go away. I usually will go away. The world is full of competitors who do possess good people skills.

TEAMWORK – PEOPLE SKILLS IN ACTION!

There is a story about a little girl who wandered away from her home and got lost among the growing wheat. Residents assembled to conduct a search for the little girl. The search was difficult, because the surrounding acres of wheat fields were vast, and the tall wheat made every square foot a potential hiding place. Several days passed and no one found the girl. Finally someone suggested that everybody should join hands and walk through the same area. This way, a better search could be conducted, since no area would be overlooked.

As the story goes, it worked. The girl was found. Unfortunately, she was dead.

A sad, simple story, but it clearly illustrates the power of teamwork, or the combining of efforts and talents to accomplish a single purpose. Each individual searched for days with no results; yet, when they acted as a single unit, they accomplished their objective (although it was too late to help the little girl).

It's amazing what can be accomplished by teamwork. For example, University of Maryland research indicates that it's a good idea to plant tomatoes and asparagus together for the mutual benefit of both crops. The reason? Asparagus kills nemotodes, a disease that attacks and destroys the roots of the tomato plants. At the same time, tomatoes repel the asparagus beetle, which feeds, quite naturally, on asparagus.

The result? Both plants together will fare better than

either plant will fare separately. That's teamwork. Applying this principle to people, a mixture of personalities will many times make each other stronger and produce a better result than the individual personalities working alone.

Of course, vegetables don't have to worry about getting along, but people do. And there is nothing that will impede the process of teamwork more than bad relationships. If people irritate or antagonize each other, they won't be able to work together either effectively or efficiently. People who can treat each other with the same respect that they would like to be afforded will produce results. It's as simple as the Golden Rule, which is what good people skills are all about.

If you can pay more attention to the input a person is giving you rather than how offensive the person seems to be to you, you will be in a better position to employ good people skills.

REQUIREMENTS FOR WORK RELATIONS

It's nice to work with people that you like. After all, some co-workers spend as much if not more time together than they spend with their families. Good friendships in the work place can make for a stronger team.

However, it's unrealistic to think that co-workers are always going to like other co-workers. The world is filled with many personalities and some personalities just don't mix.

True professionals don't let personal feelings interfere with their professional relationships. When they do, both the work lives and the individuals' personal lives suffer.

Many years ago a comedy team of two guys, Rowan and Martin, hosted "Laugh-In," a smash hit television series. They worked well together during their weekly routines. Off camera, however, they had little if anything to do with each other. While there wasn't any particular enmity or hostility cited between the two men, it was no secret that they didn't mix in their private lives. Yet, they became very successful, and presumably wealthy, thanks to teamwork and their human relations skills.

People skills can dissolve, however, and when they do teamwork usually follows suit. Dean Martin and Jerry Lewis were a successful comedy team also. Then suddenly, at the height of their popularity, they split, and it was no secret that hard feelings were the cause. The teamwork couldn't continue because the two could no longer bring themselves to employ the necessary people skills to work together harmoniously.

BE OBJECTIVE

I shouldn't have to give you advice on how to employ good people skills with people you like. It should come naturally. It's the people you don't like that may give you trouble.

Some people will simply be impossible to work with. Before you give up, try to be objective. When a co-worker or a manager whom you don't like makes a suggestion or an order that initially seems senseless or unnecessary, try to think of how you would view the suggestion or order had it been given by someone whom you like.

In short, if you can pay more attention to the input a person is giving you rather than how offensive the person seems to you, you'll be in a better position to employ good people skills. That will lead to better teamwork and success.

Of course, people skills are most important between coworkers and managers and subordinates. However, people skills are probably never more important than they are when one person meets another for the first time. When two people meet, each conducts a first-impressions test upon the other. If the test results are negative, the person judged will have a difficult time changing the other's opinion.

You get only one chance to make a good first impression. Therefore, it's most important that you don't blow it. Turn to the next chapter and I'll explain how to maximize your chances of making a good first impression.

CHAPTER SUMMARY

❖ Your ability to get along with people can either make or break you in your career. It's important that people enjoy their careers to be happy, but it's also important that they can get along with their co-workers. If they can't, problems can develop.

❖ Good people skills are essential to keeping customers. A company that places more importance on advertising than it does on people is throwing money away.

❖ The best managers are both people and task-oriented.

❖ People skills are for serving people's needs to the best of your abilities.

❖ Successful teamwork is a fine example of people skills in action.

❖ You don't have to like someone to work effectively together.

❖ If you're working with someone you don't like, be objective when receiving input from that person. This will help you maintain good people skills.

CHAPTER TWELVE

Put Your Best Foot Forward

With the exception of the time that you spend alone, your human relations skills are always at work. When you're on-the-job your people skills help you get along with your co-workers. When you're at home your people skills will help you interact positively with your family. And when you're in between the two commuting in your car your people skills will determine whether you're a courteous motorist or an ill-tempered, horn-blowing nuisance.

Whether we act good or bad toward others, we are still employing our people skills in the interacting.

When we don't behave we are employing bad people skills. I've known some people who used good people skills at work, but when they went home for the evening their spouses went to another room, the children went to their bedrooms, and the family dog went behind a sofa. Then again I've known people who were wonderful to their families, but their employees or subordinates had quite a different story to tell about them at work!

The ideal situation, of course, is to be consistent by employing good people skills in any given situation, even in your car. Some might say especially in your car! The driver to whom you offer one-half of a victory salute when he pulls out in front of you may be your friend, co-worker, boss or, worse, your minister. You never know.

When you first meet a person the impression you give them is like an unspoken exam. It is important to employ good people skills from the beginning of a new relationship. This way you don't flunk the first test.

To keep from flunking someone's first-impression test remember that good people skills begin instantly – the very second that you meet a person. Even a delay of five minutes or less in employing proper people skills may cause irreparable damage to a budding relationship. Let me explain.

GET OFF TO A GOOD START

Good people skills consist of more than just being polite. These skills involve everything you do.

For example, when you first meet someone you probably shake his or her hand. How do you like someone to shake your hand? Most people feel that an enthusiastic handshake consists of a firm grip, but not one intended to injure or cripple (a person who enjoys breaking hands isn't displaying good people skills at all).

On the other hand, I also don't like a "dead fish" handshake – one that involves nothing more than a light, limp clasp of the hand. It matters not whether the person is a man or a woman, such a grip indicates indifference and I find it difficult to be interested in someone who is indifferent to me.

Another thing that does not make for a good first impression is when someone won't smile when the occasion calls for it. And I can think of no occasion that calls for a smile as much as when one person is introduced to another. When two people meet for the first time I think a smile from both parties is only proper.

It never ceases to amaze me the people I meet who apparently disagree. I could understand it if a smile actually cost something, but that's not the case. Anyone can smile, regardless of their circumstances. In fact, it actually takes less effort to smile than it does to frown, since more muscles are used for the latter. A person who doesn't take the trouble to offer a smile when we meet is communicating the same message as the person who offers a limp handshake, and I can't help but take it personally.

A person who doesn't take the trouble to offer a smile when we meet is communicating the same message as the person who offers a limp handshake, and I can't help but to take it personally.

Of course, good grooming and appropriate posture are important to making a good first impression also, as I pointed out in the chapter on appearance. Yet, I can make concessions on those counts under certain circumstances. If a person has been up all night working on an important project or tending to a sick child I can understand how his or her appearance and posture could be affected. A firm handshake and a smile, however, are critical to establishing good human relations and should be offered no matter what the circumstance.

PEOPLE SKILLS REQUIRE GOOD BEHAVIOR

As I pointed out earlier, people remember us most when we behave the worst. If you're making a spectacle of yourself when you meet someone how do you think that person will remember you?

I heard someone say recently that the only way to change some people's cold-hearted behavior is with a heart transplant. He went on to say that if he needed a new heart he would want one from a bill collector ... because it has never been used.

Of course, that's in jest, because behavior is determined by a person's mind and attitude. It's important that we manage our behavior, then behavior can indeed be managed. Remember you can't always control what happens to you, but you most certainly can control your reactions to these things. This is important all the time, but especially when you're around new people who might be conducting first-impression tests on you.

You may perceive your behavior to be good; however, if other people hold different perceptions you might need to reevaluate your behavior. That's why I've always advised people not to discount their enemies, because enemies will tell the truth. A man who didn't particularly like me once told me that I talked too much and was a lousy listener. I thought about it and came to the conclusion that he was right.

Sometimes I have been prone to monopolize conversations. Of course, the fact that I recognized this didn't make me a saint; only when I took positive action to cut down on my conversation was I in charge of my behavior. It is only when other people's perceptions of your behavior match your own that you have your behavior under control and are in fact practicing good people skills.

THE TRUTH COMES OUT OF YOUR MOUTH

Of course, the person who criticized me wasn't very adept with people skills or he would have found another way to point out my problem instead of saying, "Arnold, you've got a big mouth!" People who have good people skills employ tact when they criticize. A tactful person can be described as someone who can step on another person's shoes and not mess up the shine.

A tactful person can be described as someone who can step on another person's shoes and not mess up the shine.

On the other hand, a person who communicates without regard as to how his or her message will be received very likely lacks good people skills. Such people often cover for this deficiency by saying, "That's the way I am. I say what I mean." (These are the people who can't understand why no one will go to lunch with them.)

Your choice of words is important. If the words you use when you speak to others would offend you if they used them in a conversation with you then you are simply choosing the wrong words. To paraphrase the Golden Rule, speak unto others as you would have others speak unto you.

You can communicate any information you like in an inoffensive manner. Certainly it may not be a pleasant task to criticize anyone, but positive feedback doesn't alienate, but rather helps. With the proper words feeback is good and can strengthen the subject of your critique. To quote a bible proverb, "Faithful are the wounds of a friend, but deceitful are the kisses of an enemy." Telling someone the truth, though uncomfortable, is what a friend does. An enemy just lets you keep on doing what you are doing no matter how unprofitable it may be for you or those around you. Or as a more common saying goes, "Feedback is the breakfast of champions." Positive feedback can be most effective if it's phrased in such a way that will amuse the listener.

With the wrong words, feedback is negative and most people will actively reject it as criticism, especially if it occurs during a first meeting. First impressions can give way later to a good relationship, but a negative first-impression is very difficult to overcome.

Finally, you should be tactful, if for no other reason because you'll make friends instead of enemies. Friends will make concessions for you when you have bad days; enemies won't. As the old saying goes, "keep your words soft and sweet; you may have to eat them."

KEEP YOUR DISTANCE

Respecting other people's space comes naturally to most people. However, there are some people who violate others' personal space, either without thinking or on purpose.

People meeting for the first time usually keep a distance of about three feet. Should they become friends or co-workers, the space can comfortably be reduced to about two feet. Should they become intimate, personal space can be six inches or less.

People who purposely violate personal space generally are trying to dominate the other person. It's a sign of aggression that generally makes the person uncomfortable and virtually never makes a good first impression. Consequently, it could place in jeopardy any potential relationship that might develop.

Keep your distance at first. Respect the other person, and he or she will respect you for it.

DRESS APPROPRIATELY

Of course if you're going to a job interview you should dress at least in the style of clothing that will be appropriate for the job you're seeking. It wouldn't hurt to dress a little better, although I wouldn't overdress. I wouldn't recommend wearing a tuxedo or evening dress to any job interview.

If you're going to a party where there will be new people, you probably wouldn't want to wear a suit unless you wanted to come off as being uptight. If the party is semi-formal or formal then anything less than a suit or tuxedo would be unacceptable.

Dress for the occasion. People will judge you by the way you dress.

BE TOLERANT

It's easy to have reservations with someone on a first meeting. Perhaps the way the person dresses may be a turn-off to you. I know I've already told you that people will judge you by the way you dress, and it's true. I'm telling you however, to try not to let minor irritations color your opinion of another person. You should do your best to present yourself in the best way, but none of us are perfect at this. Therefore you should be tolerant of people when you meet them and give them a chance even if the first impression they leave with you is not so great.

Be tolerant; give the other person a chance. Perhaps you won't wind up liking him or her. On the other hand, you just might end up as good friends. Don't flunk the other person's first-impression test by being intolerant because they may have flunked one point on your first impression test of them.

KNOW HOW TO LISTEN

One of the most important parts of a first impression will be your willingness to listen. People like to talk with people who will listen to them. When a person is speaking, the person to whom he or she is talking should be listening. If he or she isn't, it can be most disconcerting, not to mention downright rude to the speaker.

Don't flunk the other person's first-impression test by being intolerant because they may have flunked one point on your first impression test of them.

Listen well. If you seem more wrapped up in yourself than you are with the person you are meeting, you'll do yourself a disservice. First it will show and the person will judge you for it. Second, by being intensely involved in yourself you'll be missing any possible benefit that might materialize from making a good first impression. Most importantly, you are likely to miss learning something new.

There will be more on this in the next chapter.

SPEAK CLEARLY!

When it's your turn to talk, take the floor, but by all means, speak clearly! As far as I'm concerned mumbling is rude – especially if the message is important and must be heard.

Huddle Ledbetter, better known as Leadbelly, is one of the most famous folk musicians of the 20th century. The undisputed master of the twelve-string guitar, which when he played sounded like a piano, he wrote such popular songs as "Cottonfields" and "The Midnight Special." Although his performances were moving, he sang with the thick Negro dialect that originated from Louisiana and was very difficult to understand. Another popular folk singer of the same era, Josh White, who also was black, reportedly had enormous respect for Leadbelly, but at the same time was one of his harshest critics. White, who had an appreciation for good diction, sang with crisp, clear delivery that could be easily understood. He frequently criticized Leadbelly by asking, "What's the point of singing if no one can understand the words?"

I feel the same way about verbal communication. What's the point of talking if the delivery is incomprehensible? The person is only making sounds.

Enunciate your words, and make your voice strong enough to be heard. This doesn't mean that you have to learn to speak perfect unaccented English like national television news commentators, and it also doesn't mean you have to shout. It simply means to pronounce your words clearly with sufficient volume for them to be heard and understood.

KNOW HOW TO COMMUNICATE

Communication plays an important part of a first impression, especially if you have an important message for your listener. It is important to understand how communication occurs and how a person remembers the communications. Talking isn't always enough.

Even if you state your point clearly, there is a good chance your listener might not remember what you say. Statistics indicate that all the ways we learn, our sense of hearing accounts for only 11 percent of learned information. Yet, our sense of sight accounts for 83 percent of everything we learn.

Make powerful first impressions by maximizing your oral and visual communications skills when appropriate ... it will link you with another person through the bonds of effective communicaton.

Statistics also show that three hours after oral communication has occurred the listener will retain only 25 percent of the information. Three days later, the listener has retained only 10 percent

With visual communication, a listener recalls 72 percent of the information after three hours. That percentage drops to 20 percent after three days.

However, if the two forms of communication are combined – that is, if a point is made through oral and visual communication – the listener retains 85 percent of the information after three hours and 65 percent after three days.

Make powerful first impressions by maximizing your oral and visual communication skills when appropriate. Of course, this technique works just as well with old friends as it does new people. It will link you with another person through the bonds of effective communication.

Communication is an important part of people skills. The next chapter is devoted to maximizing your communication skills.

CHAPTER SUMMARY

❖ Good people skills begin the very second you meet a person.

❖ Good people skills can be discovered in the forms of a firm handshake, a smile, good grooming, proper attire and good behavior.

❖ Choice of words and tone of voice is most important in communication.

❖ Don't be labeled as overly aggressive. Respect other people's personal space.

❖ Dress appropriately for any given occasion. Neither overdress nor underdress.

❖ Although people do judge others by the way they dress, be tolerant with others. They may turn out to be good friends.

❖ Be willing to listen to others. Don't monopolize the conversation.

❖ When it's your turn to talk, speak clearly and with sufficient volume. If something is worth saying, it's worth saying well enough to be comprehended.

❖ Communication during a first meeting can be enhanced by communicating orally and visually.

CHAPTER THIRTEEN

Communication Is Essential For Success

In the classic comedy "The Pink Panther Strikes Again," Peter Sellers, as bumbling "Inspector Clouseau," learns the hard way about good and bad communication.

The Inspector is checking into an inn and passes a small dog lying on the carpet of the lobby. The ordinarily uptight Inspector smiles at the sight of the creature and kneels as he asks the innkeeper demurely, "Does your dog bite?" The innkeeper indicates "no" and the Inspector reaches out to pet the dog and is attacked, the dog gripping the fingers of Clouseau's glove and dangling a moment in mid-air as Clouseau abruptly stands. Startled and irritated, Clouseau says, "I thought you said your dog does not bite!" To which the innkeeper replies, "That is not my dog."

Good communication depends on good information and appropriate means of delivery. Shortfalls in any part can lead to misunderstanding, or worse. As in the Inspector's case it led to a dog bite!

Good communication is essential to success mainly because it's the only way a person can deliver a message to another. It matters not what sophisticated system we might have for transferral of the message, be it phone, email, video chat, or television. If the message isn't properly phrased, good communication simply won't exist.

Good communication depends on good information and appropriate means of delivery.

Good communication can be hampered by many factors. Let me review a few cases where poor communication resulted from various factors.

On a trip to Las Vegas, Nevada, my wife was shopping in a lady's clothing store when a man walked up to her and asked, "What size pants do you wear?"

My wife's initial reaction was to tell him that her pants size was none of his business. However, the surprised look on her face served as proper communication to the man that he had not given her sufficient information. He backed up a bit by saying that my wife appeared to be about the same size as his wife, for whom he wanted to buy a pair of pants – only he didn't know her size. With that explanation, my wife relaxed and willingly gave him the information he wanted.

In this case good communication was hampered by a lack of information.

Of course, there's the old joke about the airline flight reservationist who received a call from someone asking how long it would take to fly from Indianapolis to Los Angeles. The reservationist in response said, "one moment" and began to check. Instantly, the caller said, "Thank you," and hung up the phone.

How about the man who called a nurse to ask if his wife had gone into labor? The nurse asked, "Is this her first child?" The man replied, "No, this is her husband."

In the two previous scenarios, misunderstandings hampered good communication. Of course, both of these situations are humorous and probably not typical of most examples of communication failure.

Failed communication is not always a humorous matter. History books are filled with stories of terrible conflicts based on miscommunication.

In our daily lives and business lives the statistics are abundant.A survey of more than 1,000 managers, supervisors and other administrators indicated that 30 percent of all on-the-job problems boiled down to poor communication. I know some managers who would place the percentage at 90 percent – or higher.

There are many reasons why people fail to communicate properly. Here are ten of them.

Prejudice.

The listener has concluded – either before or during the speaker's remarks – that the speaker has nothing significant to say. The reasons for such prejudice are many. Perhaps it could be the speaker's appearance, age, actions, voice, race, religion or nationality to mention a few.

Jumping to conclusions.

The listener has decided that what the speaker is saying is too difficult, too trite, too boring or otherwise unsuited to his or her needs. Therefore, the listener feigns attentiveness while his or her mind is elsewhere.

Assumption.

Many times, listeners assume they already know what the speaker is going to say, so their attention drifts elsewhere. As a result, they miss the new information the speaker may give.

Closed mind.

When the listener decides that he or she already knows what the speaker is going to say, the listener simply decides not to listen.

Inattention.

Most people speak about 125 words per minute, while they can think at a rate of between 500 and 1,000 words per minute. As a result, many listeners use the "spare time" to think of what they are going to say next. In the process, listeners often miss out on much of what the speaker says.

Selective listening.

Listeners sometimes hear only what they want to hear. This is especially true with children and some teen-agers.

Different meanings.

Many words have varied meanings. For example, the word "slug" can mean a crawling creature, a bullet, a swallow of a drink, a punch in the face or a counterfeit coin. Likewise, the word "ring" could be the sound of a bell, a metal band worn around the finger, a group of people organized to commit crimes, a telephone call or a line of dirt that encircles the bathtub or, thanks to modern culture, a shirt collar. Sometimes, the listener can be confused, especially if the speaker doesn't make clear precisely what he or she intends to say.

Excessive talking.

If a "listener" insists on monopolizing the conversation, he or she isn't going to hear very much. I was taken to task for this one, remember?

Lack of empathy.

Sometimes, a person cannot or will not see both sides of a point. Dogmatic people generally are poor listeners. They don't have the ability to, or desire to, put themselves in the other person's situation.

Fear.

When a listener suspects that a speaker is about to prove him or her wrong, fear may result. Many times, he or she might stop listening and find a way to start an argument as a means of not admitting being wrong.

To be a good listener, learn these ten reasons for lack of communication and try to be aware of them, especially if you find your listening skills hampered by them. To get along in this world, a person must be able to listen properly.

SAY WHAT YOU MEAN!

Breakdowns in communications aren't always the fault of the listener. Often the speaker fails to deliver his or her point properly.

"A man's power to connect his thought with its proper symbol, and so to utter it, depends upon the simplicity of his character– that is, upon his love of truth and his desire to communicate it without loss."

The preceding paragraph isn't original. Instead, it was written by the wise philosopher Ralph Waldo Emerson. I'll agree with him, except to say that it applies to women as well.

People often say things they don't mean, and mean things they don't say. So, say what you mean so your listeners will actually hear what you want to say.

Say what you mean so your listeners will actually hear what you want to say.

Speaking is like behavior. Just because a person knows what he or she intends to say doesn't mean that he or she has delivered the point. Only when the listeners' perceptions of the message match those of the speaker has good communication occurred.

SOME SPEAKERS TURN OFF!

Finally, another reason why good communication often doesn't occur can be traced to the attitude of the speaker.

There are three types of communicators – aggressive, non-assertive and assertive. Two of the three aren't very effective; the non-agressive and the aggressive.

Whenever I explain the difference between the three – especially the difference between aggressive and non-aggressive – I can't help but think of the times when I was a child.

When I was a child in my hometown of Beattyville, Kentucky, my mother would take me to town while she did the weekly shopping. One particularly hot Saturday afternoon we walked downtown toward the grocery store, passing by the ice cream parlor. I just happened to glance into the window and saw a woman behind the counter gingerly positioning two huge scoops of strawberry ice cream atop a brown sugar cone. The sight was too much to behold. I asked my mother to buy me an ice cream cone, but she flatly refused, leading me instead toward the grocery store.

Of course, I was disappointed that I didn't get any ice cream. So I decided my best course of action would be to hang my head in sorrow and mope along like a wounded puppy, hoping my mother would feel the shame of having denied me an afternoon snack and reconsider her position. My non-assertive attitude didn't work with my mother. In fact, being nonassertive rarely, if ever, produces the desired results.

So I changed my strategy. I decided that I would become assertive, telling my mother every reason in the world why I should have an ice cream cone. It would make me happy to eat something sweet and cold on such a hot day, it would ease my hunger and, since ice cream is mostly milk anyway, it would be nutritious for me, I told her.

That didn't work, either. Mothers can be tough nuts to crack. So that left only one option – aggression.

When my mother and I crossed Main Street in Beattyville to go to the grocery store, I simply stopped when we reached the yellow line dividing the highway. To make sure she got the message, I lay down on the street and refused to budge until she promised me that I would get an ice cream cone.

Sometimes, aggression works. That day in Beattyville, I discovered that aggression would work for me. In the years that followed, I resorted to aggression whenever I wanted something. I'm not proud of this fact, but it is true.

Later, I was to learn a hard lesson: Aggression often backfires.

AGGRESSION IS FOR FOOLS

Aggression may indeed produce the desired results, but not without a cost. First, even if an aggressive message ("Do this or else!") does produce results, the listener is not going to feel good about the speaker. No one likes to be ordered. An aggressive messenger has little or no regard for the feelings of the listener; the messenger puts his wants and needs first. If the listener produces the desired results, it's usually out of fear of what may result (loss of job, physical assault, blackmail) and not out of respect for the speaker. Virtually always, aggressive speakers genuinely earn the contempt of their listeners.

A big part of breaking any mediocre routine or bad habit involves filling the void with a successful routine and a good habit.

Second, aggression doesn't work all of the time. Some listeners will reject aggression or, worse yet, meet aggression with aggression. This is how most arguments and wars begin; pride often fuels the conflicts long after the cause has been forgotten.

Third, aggression virtually never produces good long-term results. Let me explain.

I recall an incident when I learned a hard lesson about people skills. A man who worked for me was assigned to make a personal collection call on a night when he chose instead to take his wife to a movie. When the man came in the next day, I asked him if he had made the collection call. He told me he had not. In anger, I slammed down a telephone receiver I happened to be holding at the time with such force that it broke not only the telephone, but a wristwatch I was wearing as well.

The man got my point. He instantly headed out the door and made the collection call. My aggression message had worked.

Several days later, he sent an assertive message to me by quitting his job. I had lost a good collector, and I knew exactly why I lost him. Furthermore, I knew that every one else in the office also knew why he left. Under the circumstances, I couldn't blame him for leaving.

ASSERTIVE SPEAKERS GET BEST RESULTS

Had I been assertive instead of aggressive I might have had better results. An assertive message straightforwardly states the desires of the messenger without belittling the rights of the listener. Of course, I had a right to be angry at the collector for failing to do as I had asked, but there were other, more positive ways to handle the situation than to make a spectacle of myself at his expense. Instead of slamming down the phone and drawing the attention of everyone in the office, I should have said, "Come into my office. We need to talk." Then I could have expressed my expectations and ultimatums in a forthright manner without resorting to intimidation.

Of course, the opposite of assertive is non-assertive. I've never been accused of being non-assertive, and I doubt I ever will be. A non-assertive speaker has no regard for his or her own feelings. For example, suppose I used a non-assertive message with the collector upon learning he had not made the collection call as I had asked. I might have said, "If you'd rather not, perhaps another collector can do it instead. Would you like for me to see if another collector is free?"

An assertive message straightforwardly states the desires of the messenger without belittling the rights of the listener.

A non-assertive speaker makes it easy for people to use him or her for a doormat. Such speakers don't respect themselves, so few if anyone else will respect them, either.

A FABLE FOR THOUGHT

The proper attitude for anyone wishing to communicate is illustrated in a fable about the Wind and the Sun. One day, the Wind and the Sun were watching a man walking by the side of a road, his cloak wrapped tightly about him. The Wind challenged the Sun to a contest to determine which one of them could first get the cloak off the man. The Wind, being the blustery soul that it was, boasted that it could remove the cloak by literally blowing it off. The Sun just smiled and predicted that the Wind would fail.

The Wind got the first try. It blew great gusts of air directly toward the man, who was virtually knocked over by its force. Still, the cloak remained, mainly because the man clutched it tightly. The Wind became angry. Summoning all the strength it could muster, the Wind offered its best shot. The man was actually knocked down by the powerful blast of air, but his cloak stayed with him, his grip becoming tighter than ever.

The Wind was exhausted. The Sun still smiled. So the Wind told the Sun to try, doubting that the Sun would be able to do anything that it was unable to do itself. But the Sun's smile never faded. Instead, the Sun immediately began to shine brightly. As a result, the man relaxed his tight grip on the cloak. The Sun's rays increased in intensity, becoming much warmer, until the man finally removed the cloak altogether.

The Sun had won, but not because of bluster or force. Instead, the Sun appealed to the man on his own terms by motivating him to take off his coat for his own reasons – because he was getting hot.

SHINE LIKE THE SUN

Aggressive speakers are like the Wind. They figuratively try to blow down listeners, intimidating them with insults or ridicule for their positions. Of course, if the listeners are as aggressive as the speakers, the exchange of messages is likely to escalate into a shouting match.

Assertive speakers are like the Sun. They know how to create the right climate for the listener to receive their points. Their words, which are friendly and courteous, are the warmth they use to "turn up the heat a bit" on the listener to make him or her want to drop any prejudices he or she might hold.

In short, when communicating, always respect the listener,

but not at the expense of your own self-respect. In so doing, you'll create the ideal climate for good communication.

Sometimes, this takes courage, especially if your listener is particularly stubborn, irate or physically intimidating. Sometimes, it takes courage not only to communicate well, but to succeed, also.

I'll explain this in the next and last chapter of this book.

CHAPTER SUMMARY

❖ Good communication is indeed essential to success, mainly because its the only way a person can deliver a message to another.

❖ There are many reasons why people fail to communicate properly. They include prejudice, jumping to conclusions, assumptions, closed mind, inattention, selective listening, different meanings, excessive talking, lack of empathy and fear.

❖ Say what you mean. Some miscommunication results from the speaker incorrectly phrasing what he or she intends to say.

❖ The attitude of the speaker can turn-off many listeners. Aggressive and non-assertive speakers often have hostile or inattentive listeners. An assertive message is best for good communication.

SECTION FIVE
Courage

Courage: Willingness to pursue goals in the face of uncertainty.

The Inukshuk is the symbol for the 2010 Olympic games in Vancouver, British Columbia, Canada. The Inukshuk was selected as the symbol for these Olympics to speak to the entire wealth of this ancient emblem in symbolizing friendship, community, sanctity of life, and the courage to succeed. The inukshuk spans time and is a symbol of the quest of people everywhere to find success. Not just success, but significant success. The inukshuk is the symbol of the quest of the human spirit for meaning, the desire to reach our ultimate destination. In ancient times and today it takes courage to set out from the village for the hunt, keep going in difficult times, and remember it is not the hunt that is important but what the hunt gives to the hunter to bring back home. It takes courage from beginning to end.

CHAPTER FOURTEEN

It Takes Courage To Succeed

A quote often attributed to the conqueror Napoleon is, "Imagination rules the world." I rather think it is courage that does the ruling. Without courage a person doesn't dare imagine some of the dreams that come to guide their lives, whether positive or negative.

Of the four success traits I've presented in this book, which would you think is the most important characteristic that separates successful people from failures?

Many people might think dedication is most important. Charting a specific course of action and devoting yourself to following it is a necessary ingredient to success. Yet, many dedicated people fail to reach their destinations because they get sidetracked during their trips.

Some people might think self-belief is important. Yet, belief is probably the most fragile ingredient of success. The world is full of critics and mediocre people who would discourage you. As a result, your belief system may shatter like a piece of glass dropped upon a concrete floor.

Self-control must be the most important quality, right? After all, if a person can control his or her actions, he or she could do almost anything, right? Yet, if a person's dedication and belief fades, self-control is apt to do likewise. After all, the incentive to control your actions is likely to fade fast if you don't know where you're going and seriously doubt you could get there, even if you did.

Could people skills be the most important trait supporting success? Not by a long shot. The world is full of nice, polite failures.

The fact of the matter is simple. None of the four traits is any more – nor any less – important than the other. If one trait diminishes, at least one of the other four is likely to diminish with it.

However, there is a character trait that separates successful people from failures. With this trait, a person can maintain his or her dedication, belief, control and people skills even during times of extreme discouragement.

This trait is courage. It takes courage to succeed, because courage is what pulls together the previous four ingredients of success.

Courage is what will make you maintain your dedication at times when you'd rather not. When you are tired and scared. It will help you nurture your belief system at times when the world seems to ridicule you for trying, and when even you believe you might fail. Courage will help you keep going. It will help you keep control when your every fiber wants to run amok. It will help you maintain your people skills at times when you'd rather explode and tell that obstinate so-and-so who is the cause of your headache to swallow an Alka-Seltzer – without water.

To put it simply, successful people take courage to put into practice all the other traits when everything about them says the only logical thing to do is to let go and quit.

NOTHING VENTURED, NOTHING GAINED

To undertake anything involves the risk of failure. Mediocre people tend to shy away from failure by not trying. Successful people tend to shy away from failure by trying ... and trying and trying. Sooner or later, they're bound to make it.

Successful people are motivated by long-term pleasures, which generally involve short-term discomforts. They're willing to endure the discomforts because they have courage. Failures tend to favor short-term pleasures that generally involve long-term discomforts. Then the time comes to endure the long-term discomforts, one of two things usually happen.

Successful people are motivated by long-term pleasures, which generally involve short-term discomforts.

In the first alternative, the failures become bitter. They look everywhere for someone to blame. If they can find no one, they'll blame their circumstances. In any event, they'll simply accept their situations and endure – not enjoy – the rest of their lives.

The other alternative? They'll get tired of being failures and start doing things it will take to be successful. By accepting the reality of their shortcomings, they'll strengthen their resolve never to have to endure long-term discomforts again.

In short, they'll develop courage. Rather than blame the world for their lack of success, they'll blame themselves. That indeed takes courage. Then they'll dedicate themselves to develop the self-discipline to make better lives for themselves.

SELF-DISCIPLINE REQUIRES COURAGE

If your lifestyle is not conducive to success, then a change in lifestyle is in order. Of course, that's easier said than done.

It's difficult to break a long-established routine, especially one that's filled with habits that aren't conducive to success. As it has been said before, the chains of habit are too weak to be felt until they are too strong to be broken.

Human beings are creatures of habit. It's extremely difficult to break a routine with which one has become comfortable. People who are accustomed to sleeping late, excessive on-the-job socializing and watching too much television often find it difficult to change their non-productive habits. They fear taking on a new lifestyle because they perceive it to be uncomfortable at best and demanding

> **The chains of habits are too weak to be felt until they are too strong to be broken.**

at worst. Yet, those who are successful in adopting a new routine usually find that, in the words of Franklin Delano Roosevelt, "there was nothing to fear except fear itself."

Breaking any bad habit requires courage, especially if the habit is physically or psychologically addictive. Sometimes, a person might need help in overcoming a nicotine addiction, an alcohol and/or drug dependence or a weight problem. Seeking and accepting professional counseling to overcome these problems requires courage.

As a society, we're becoming more health conscious than ever before. Yet, we still tend to practice what many physicians consider to be poor health habits. According to a survey, 58 percent of the American people don't exercise regularly, 31 percent smoke regularly, 29 percent indulge in excessive drinking, 28 percent are chronically overweight, 25 percent routinely skip breakfast and 22 percent sleep less than seven hours each night.

Why do people continue to practice bad health habits when they know that there is a big price to pay? Many times they don't know how to break a bad habit. A big part of breaking any mediocre routine or bad habit involves filling the void with a successful routine and a good habit, and it indeed takes courage to adopt a good habit.

To attempt a new lifestyle requires courage, because it generally will mean that some comfortable practice must be sacrificed. Probably the toughest new lifestyle to adopt is one that involves a tighter rein on your financial expenditures. It takes courage to live by a budget.

Yet, many people don't have this courage. While Japanese people save 20 percent of their disposable income, the average American consumer devotes all 18 percent of his or her income to installment debts. This percentage is at an all-time high, and it does not include mortgage payments!

Instead of saving and investing for their future, these people often exchange their future income for the pleasures of today. Of course, when they're still paying bills years later to pay for the pleasures of yesterday, they can become bitter, because the future becomes a financial nightmare.

Wouldn't it have been better if these people could have avoided this by having taken the time in the past to dream for a better future?

If you find yourself in this category, it's not too late.

DREAM BIG THEN WORK!

It doesn't take courage to dream big dreams. To work to bring those dreams to reality, however, requires a great deal of courage, because there usually will be no shortage of people to tell you that you're wasting your time.

It takes courage to act, simply because inaction is easier.

Critics told Robert Fulton that he was crazy, but that didn't discourage him. He produced the steamboat and everyone who had called it "Fulton's Folly" had to eat his or her words.

Critics told Christopher Columbus that he was crazy to attempt a trans-ocean voyage on the belief that the world was round. Everyone knew that the world was flat, they said, and Columbus would fall off the side of the earth into infinity – if he and his crew weren't first devoured by sea monsters. In retrospect, who seems crazy – Columbus or his critics?

Critics told Margaret Mitchell she lacked the depth to

write a book worthy of publishing. Readers throughout the world who have enjoyed *Gone With The Wind* will disagree.

All of these people had courage to announce their goals. You'll need courage to announce your goal if there are any critics in your life (and there probably are). My question to you is, will you let critics talk you out of being successful?

Don't waste energy trying to defend your goals to your critics. Use that energy instead to work to bring your dreams to reality.

The best advice I can give anyone is to work long and hard. Stay overworked and underpaid. That way, you'll always have a job. Furthermore, be willing to do what others don't want to do. My willingness to collect debts – a job that so many find to be distasteful – has helped me to enjoy what success I have achieved.

People who fail often aren't willing to work more than eight hours per day, forty hours per week. They're too busy pursuing short-term pleasures to put in overtime. Successful people are willing to work as long as it takes to get the job done. They know that this is the only route to success, and no matter how long the route may be, they have the courage to travel it.

Successful people are motivated by their dreams of a better way of life. Others merely wish a better way of life would happen.

IT TAKES COURAGE TO ACT

It takes courage to act, simply because inaction is easier. Taking action requires effort; inaction doesn't. Taking action involves risk of failure. Inaction involves no risk at all; the results of inaction are sure and certain. Taking action also requires courage because someone, somewhere will criticize, while inaction cannot be critiqued.

Whenever you take action on anything new, you run not only the risk of failure, but the risk of possible embarrassment as well, because you're likely to do it badly at first. That takes courage.

It also takes courage to build a belief system. Remember the four stages of belief that we covered – unconscious incompetent, conscious incompetent, conscious competent and unconscious competent? It takes courage to experience each step, even the first one, but especially to be willing to persist beyond the conscious incompetent stage. Successful people experience each phase. Others quit at the conscious incompetent stage because they lack the courage to continue.

No one enjoys criticism, but successful people must have it to grow.

IT TAKES COURAGE TO SEEK CRITIQUES

No one enjoys criticism, but successful people must have it to grow. Therefore, successful people seek out critiques of their work, and they take the criticism in good spirit. This indeed takes courage, for it is easier to operate under the assumption that your work has no room for improvement. Many failures I know have extremely high opinions of themselves – too high, in fact, to be rooted in reality.

Successful people seek critiques for other important matters. It takes courage to ask someone to rate you as a parent, as a friend, as a fellow club or organization member or for your people skills.

I hired a full-time psychologist for American Accounts Collection Agency, Inc. Steve Tranbarger is indeed an asset to the company, since calling delinquent debtors to collect past-due accounts can lead to stress and frustration in employees with which a psychologist can help them cope. I also hired Steve to critique me on my people skills. Sometimes, he didn't always say what I wanted to hear, but if he had, he wouldn't have been doing his job. It took courage to listen to his critiques, but I'd like to think I'm a better person for having done it.

IT TAKES COURAGE TO GET UP AFTER A FALL

Of course the road to success can be rough at times. Honest criticism and hidden pitfalls can challenge your belief system and cause you to stumble. Successful people don't mind falling because they will get up and resume their travels. That takes courage, too.

It takes courage to drive again after wrecking a car. In 1966, I was enroute to Texas on an interstate when a horse stepped out in front of me. I hit the horse and wrecked my car. I got it sufficiently repaired to drive, and, believe me, it took courage for me to drive after having a wreck, but I did.

On my way home the next day my car ran off the road and over a hill. You'd better believe it took courage for me to drive again after my second accident within two days.

The world is full of people who failed then who became successful because they were willing to keep trying. R.H. Macy opened seven stores that failed before his New York store finally made it big – Macy's Department Store, which still operates today. British novelist John Creasey got 753 rejection slips before he was able to publish his 564 books. Baseball's famous Babe Ruth struck out 1,330 times – a record for strikeouts, but he also hit 714 home runs, a record that was not broken until the mid 1970s by Hank Aaron.

One of America's biggest successes – Walt Disney – started out with many failures, but he was willing to try again. The classic animated films and his famous theme parks will attest to his success.

"All the adversity I've had in my life, all my troubles and obstacles have strengthened me," Disney once said. "It is good to have a failure while you're young because it teaches you so much. For one thing it makes you aware that such a thing can happen to anybody, and once you've lived through the worst, you're never quite as vulnerable afterward. You may not realize it when it happens, but a kick in the teeth may be the best thing in the world for you."

It takes courage to try, and it takes more courage to try again after failing. Such is the path that leads to success.

THE COURAGEOUS STAND UP FOR BELIEFS

When you believe in something, you must live by your beliefs. Successful people stand up for their beliefs; others stand up for what is beneficial to them at the moment.

I've turned down bookings for seminars because the clients asked me not to speak of my love for Christ. That took courage. Likewise, it took courage to take criticism because of my love for Christ, or to be disliked because of my refusal to support all types of so-called Christian or church works because I could financially.

It also took courage to avoid taverns with friends and

clients because I didn't think the atmosphere was conducive to successful living. It took courage to avoid certain movies and television shows because I didn't think the content was the least bit enriching. It took courage to excuse myself because of bad language, or to dismiss associates for using bad language or for their bad habits.

It also took courage to avoid particular business deals because it went against the grain of my belief. Once, I refused to sell property I owned because the buyers wanted to put a liquor store on the property. I felt that it wasn't best for the town.

Successful people stand up for their beliefs; others stand up for what is beneficial to them at the moment.

I could go on and on with my beliefs, but I think I've offered enough examples. I'm not trying so much to say that your beliefs must match mine before you'll be successful. I'm saying that you must stand up for whatever you believe. That will take courage.

COURAGEOUS PEOPLE

Perhaps you've already started your success journey. If you have, happy traveling! If you haven't, what reason do you have that's holding you back? The world is filled with people who could hardly be blamed for not being successful, yet they are anyway. Let me tell you about a few.

Helen Keller, though blind, deaf, and mute, couldn't have been blamed for not being successful. In fact, who could have blamed her for feeling sorry for herself? Deprived of the senses of which people depend for the most basic forms of communication, it would have been easy for her to have lived her life as a near-vegetable. Instead, she kept busy by learning and writing 27 books! She dedicated her life to inspiring people all over the world to become better than they are.

That took courage.

When Shirley Price was born, the doctor who delivered her put her in a shoe box and placed the lid over it. When her mother asked for her child, the doctor replied, "You don't want this baby; it's handicapped."

Shirley Price was born without hands. With only stubs for arms, she doesn't view herself as handicapped; instead, she sees herself only as being "different."

"The word handicapped used to offend me," she told an Associated Press reporter in 1985. "I don't think that's what I am. Even from a physical sense, with the skills I have, I just don't buy it."

Despite the absence of hands, Ms. Price is able to dress and groom herself, drive a car, type on a typewriter or word processor, write and feed herself. She uses her feet and toes for hands and fingers.

She came to have a job that many able-bodied people would love to have. She became a coordinator at the Equal Opportunities Office of Johnson Space Center in Houston, Texas. As well she has held various other jobs with the National Aeronautics and Space Administration facility. In addition, she earned a master's degree while working full time and was on the verge of completing her doctorate degree in 1985.

Ms. Price does some things with her feet better than some people can do them with their hands. For example, while many people have a difficult time inserting contact lenses, Ms. Price can put them in and remove them with ease.

All this was accomplished by a woman who, had she not been wanted, might have been left to die as an infant in a shoebox. That took courage.

THE REAL FAILURE IS IN NOT TRYING

The Challenger crew tried for success. They aimed for the stars, and although their failure cost them their very lives they'll not be remembered for failing to achieve what they aimed for, but for their success in bringing them to the place of their attempt. It took a lot of dedication and courage for each of them to earn a bearth on that shuttle.

What price must you pay for your attempt to succeed? Is it so great that you won't try for success? The penalty for failure wasn't great enough to deter the Challenger crew. Nor was it for the Chicago Bears. They, too, had to risk failure and possible embarrassment in their quest for success.

The Challenger crew and the Chicago Bears had courage to pull together all the other traits that success requires – dedication, belief, self-control, and people skills. Each crew and team member worked well together to pursue a common goal. One group achieved their goal; the other, though they may have failed in the most tragic sense at reaching their goal, succeeded in making the best attempt.

Success isn't necessarily a reward you will get for doing all the things it will take to be successful. As I said earlier, outside forces over which you have no control can thwart your chances of success. For that reason alone, if for no other, it takes courage to shoot for success.

Yet, a person who does what it takes to be successful will

still enjoy a better lifestyle, regardless of whether or not he or she becomes successful. Practicing good habits is its own reward; time and effort devoted to good physical, mental, emotional and spiritual pursuits is never wasted.

If you haven't already, give it a try. You'll see for yourself why Zig Ziglar says that instead of paying a price for success, you actually enjoy the price of success.

You can have a chance to be successful, too, if you're willing to enjoy the price. If you have the courage to enjoy yourself by engaging in productive habits, you'll be a success no matter how many "failures" you experience. If you can make that your minimum, daily goal, everything else will be extra! It all depends on your courage

CHAPTER SUMMARY

❖ It takes courage to succeed, because courage is what pulls together the previous four ingredients of success.

❖ Successful people do what failures won't. That takes courage. They have the courage to forego short-term pleasures for long-term rewards.

❖ Successful people have the courage to be self-disciplined.

❖ Successful people have the courage to work to accomplish big goals. It takes courage to act, simply because inaction is easier.

❖ Successful people seek out criticism to grow.

❖ Successful people also have courage to get up after they've fallen. They persist until they succeed.

❖ Successful people have the courage to stand up for their beliefs.

❖ Successful people know it's better to try and fail than never to try at all. Instead of paying the price for success, they enjoy it.

EPILOGUE

On the morning of Saturday, May 16, 1986, I experienced my first skydive, a risk goal I set for the year. Diving from 9,000 feet above the fertile farmlands of Indiana, I applied the principles covered in this book, *Common Sense Success.* You see, I made a tandem freefall!

I could have spent a great deal of time, energy and expense on ground and air instruction. Instead, I took the minimum amount of risk with the maximum amount of reward. After only 15 minutes of training using a special rig designed with two harnesses packed with a colorful square parachute, twice as large as usual, Tandem Jumpmaster, Art Cross, and "Passenger," Bill Arnold, jumped from the wing of a single engine prop plane going 120 miles per hour. Jumping over the "friendly" skies of Frankfort, Indiana, Municipal Airport, we landed on target!It was the thrill of a lifetime, just like the brochure had advertised!

I arrived at the airport in the middle of the cornfield on a beautiful spring morning. Meeting with Mark Schlatter, owner of Parachutes & Associates, who would also jump as my official flight photographer, we discussed what to expect as I signed a few release forms. Within 15 minutes I would be "airborne."

As we talked, on the bulletin board, I noticed the clippings from an article about the skydiver who had been knocked unconscious, but rescued by another gallant diver on a recent skydive attempt. I recalled an associate who witnessed a colleague plunge to his death when his chute "failed" to open ending her attraction to skydiving. Undaunted, I signed those papers and braced myself for what was going to be a fantastic experience. After all, God and I both knew I wasn't going to die! Besides, as Mark explained, I was safer in the air that morning than I was driving to and from the airport. And, Mark had never even seen me drive!

Small acts often have great consequences – if you will take action.

When we were aboard the plane, I truly had no fear, only anticipation. I had always seen war movies with soldiers jumping over war-torn Europe from planes using static lines. But, as this was a tandem jump, Art & I climbed out onto the wing of the plane, and rolled off to a freefall, falling at 100 miles per hour. It seemed like 1,000! Recording my reactions on a tape recorder strapped to my jumpsuit, my first words were, "Oh, man!" (Neil Armstrong was not going to out-quote me.) "This is unbelievable; this is great!" It was.

After freefalling to 4,500 feet, Art opened the big two-man parachute. When the chute first opened, I felt the pull back from the freedom of the fall. Gliding down, I readied for a soft stand-up landing, knees together, like sliding into home plate.

My inspiration, the great goal-setter, John Goddard, has said that if you are alive you must take risks. I took the risk to accomplish this goal. The thrill of jumping and freefalling in tandem was better than if I had done it on my own. I used the principles of *Common Sense Success*. It was the quickest and safest way to accomplish the goal. I would do it again, because the risk is worth the excitement you get!

Like much of this book, this story illustrates a simple goal. In my life there have been many other, much larger goals I have undertaken as well. Some of them have exacted a lot from me, both in courage and in exhaustion. From starting and selling several international companies to traveling to more than one hundred countries, territories and U.S. states, I have practiced in my life what I have preached in this book and I can tell you these simple ideas work.

NOW YOU HAVE A PLAN

Now you have the plan. What will you do with it?

Whether you enjoyed the book isn't so important to me as whether you'll take the principles to heart. You have within your hands the plan that can lead you to success; you have within your mind the decision to start your journey.

Don't let fear of the unknown postpone your plans indefinitely. Success isn't so much a leap over a great chasm as it is a series of small steps to a destination. There is no better day to start down your path of common sense success than this very day!

The following poem sums it up quite well:

For want of a nail, the shoe was lost.
For want of a shoe, the horse was lost.
For want of a horse, the rider was lost.
For want of a rider, the battle was lost.
For want of the battle, the kingdom was lost.
All for the want of a horseshoe nail.

Small acts often have great consequences – if you will take action.

Be prepared to make a life-long commitment to be successful. Success is a journey, not an event. It's extremely difficult, if not impossible, to achieve success without living a successful life.

Like it says in the Christian Bible, success has a lot to do with self-control. Anyone who would manage anything – especially other people – must first be able to manage himself or herself. People would much rather see a sermon than hear one.

If you would manage other people, you must first manage yourself. You can do both if you'll follow this plan and remember to treat others the way you expect to be treated yourself. Make no demands that you wouldn't make of yourself. When you can successfully manage yourself, there's no limit to what you can do.

Let me sum up what I feel success is:

Success is speaking words of praise
and cheering other people's ways.
Success is doing the best you can
with every task and every plan.

It's silence when your speech would hurt,
Politeness when your neighbor's curt.
It's loyalty when duty calls.
It's courage when disaster falls.
It's in the silent time of prayer,
In happiness and despair,
In all of life and nothing less,
We find this thing we call success.

In closing, I'd like to leave you with the same words a friend of mine tells his wife every time she goes to the beauty parlor: Good luck to you!

Visit

www.commonsensesuccess.net

Read the blog!

Bill Arnold offers the following products and services:

BOOKS BY BILL ARNOLD

Make Them Happy, Make Them Pay: A Common Sense Approach to debt recovery.

Common Sense Success: A Refresher Course on the Fundamentals of Business and Life.

Effective Collectors Guide

SEMINARS

How To Overcome Excuses

How To Negotiate For Payment-in-Full

How To Write Effective Collection Letters

The Secrets of Locating Past-Due Debtors

How To Stay Positive As A Collector

How To Set And Achieve Collection Goals

How To Locate Past-Due Accounts

How To Collect Past-Due Accounts

How To Achieve Excellence In Collections

How To Write Effective Collection Letters

For more information contact:

Inukshuk Success Press:
1586 Main Street, Southlake, TX 76092
Email: *info@commonsensesuccess.net*

817.366.9671

About The Author

Bill Arnold is an author and consultant specializing in employee development for Fortune 100 companies. His books include: **Common Sense Success:** *A refresher course on the fundamentals for business and life;* The bestseller, **Make Them Happy, Make Them Pay:** *A common sense guide to collecting past due accounts;* and **Who Cuts Your Hair and Who Serves Your Pancakes:** *A common sense approach to sharing your faith.*

Bill Arnold's materials are gleaned from decades of personal and professional success. With his companies American Accounts, Kappa Financial, and now Bill Arnold Associates, he has learned that companies succeed who develop successful employees. Bill Arnold's roster of clients includes world giants Microsoft, American Express, Target, Citibank, Shell Oil, and General Electric, to name a few.

Bill has traveled to 129 countries and territories, visiting all seven continents. He has presented more than two thousand seminars in nearly a dozen countries, including China, Australia, Chile, India, Italy, Philippines, Guatemala, United States, Canada, and Singapore.

Bill holds an honorary doctorate from Freed Hardeman University in Tennesse.

LaVergne, TN USA
30 May 2010
184470LV00002B/1/P

9 780615 232058